Issues
and
Elections

D1602935

TRANSFORMING AMERICAN POLITICS SERIES
Lawrence C. Dodd, Series Editor

Dramatic changes in political institutions and behavior over the past two decades have underscored the dynamic nature of American politics, confronting political scientists with a new and pressing intellectual agenda.

Transforming American Politics is dedicated to documenting these changes, reinterpreting conventional wisdoms, tracing historical patterns of change, and asserting new theories to clarify the direction of contemporary politics.

TITLES IN THIS SERIES

Issues
and
Elections

PRESIDENTIAL VOTING
IN CONTEMPORARY AMERICA—
A REVISIONIST VIEW

Euel W. Elliott

Westview Press
BOULDER, SAN FRANCISCO, AND LONDON

Transforming American Politics

This Westview softcover edition is printed on acid-free paper and bound in softcovers that carry the highest rating of the National Association of State Textbook Administrators, in consultation with the Association of American Publishers and the Book Manufacturers' Institute.

Published in 1989 in the United States of America by Westview Press, Inc., 5500 Central Avenue, Boulder, Colorado 80301, and in the United Kingdom by Westview Press, Inc., 13 Brunswick Centre, London WC1N 1AF, England

Library of Congress Cataloging-in-Publication Data
Elliott, Euel W., 1951– .
  Issues and elections: presidential voting in contemporary
America—a revisionist view / Euel W. Elliott.
    p. cm.—(Transforming American politics)
  Includes index.
  ISBN 0-8133-7633-5
  1. Presidents—United States—Election—1972. 2. Presidents—
United States—Election—1976. 3. Presidents—United States—
Election—1980. 4. Presidents—United States—Election—1984.
I. Title. II. Series.
JK524.E38 1989
324.973'092—dc19   88-35705
                                                                              CIP

Printed and bound in the United States of America

The paper used in this publication meets the requirements of the American National Standard for Permanence of Paper for Printed Library Materials Z39.48-1984.

10   9   8   7   6   5   4   3   2   1

Contents

Tables

Figures

Acknowledgments

It would be virtually impossible to acknowledge everyone who has assisted me in this project. So many people have provided generous amounts of their time in reviewing and critiquing all or parts of this work. My greatest debt, however, is to Allan Kornberg, at Duke University, who provided invaluable advice and criticism (out of which came this work), and to Harold Clarke, now at the University of North Texas, who originally suggested this project and contributed a tremendous amount of time to reading and rereading successive chapter drafts. Harold was also an indefatigable source of encouragement and support between 1984–1987 when I was teaching full-time while working on the manuscript.

I would also like to thank Marianne Stewart for her invaluable assistance in improving the overall style and structure of the work. Like Harold, Marianne was a major source of support during the time I was writing the original drafts. Several individuals did yeoman's work in typing successive drafts of the manuscript and later in preparing the revisions for the book. I especially want to thank Rose Zuk, Debra Harmon, and Geri Rowden for their great skill and good humor in typing frequently indecipherable manuscripts. Last, but certainly not least, I wish to thank Sally Furgeson at Westview Press for her herculean efforts on my behalf as well as her patience in the face of so many missed deadlines.

Euel W. Elliott

1

Introduction

Perhaps the first question anyone reasonably familiar with the study of electoral behavior would ask upon seeing the title of this book is "Why on earth another study of voting behavior?" This very question, however, reveals what I consider to be a fundamental problem with much of the literature in this subfield. Most political scientists working in the area of voting studies have been almost exclusively concerned with explaining the determinants of individual-level voting behavior. Indeed, studies of voting behavior have become one of the major growth industries in political science over the last several years. Political scientists have tended to ignore, at least until recently, questions concerning the dynamics and determinants of election outcomes. There is a difference between determining what factors contribute to individual voting choice in a particular election, on the one hand, and determining those factors that affect the candidate or party who actually wins the election, on the other. Indeed, a close reading of some of the voting behavior literature hints at possible confusion by using individual-level analyses to explain election outcomes. This, of course, is totally unjustified. *Issues and Elections* was written to address this deficiency. Basically, I ask: "Why does one election differ from another?" or "What explains party X winning one election and losing to party Y in the subsequent election?" A related question is "How are those factors that are important in explaining individual-level voting behavior capable of explaining the overall election outcome?" My chief contention is that factors influential at the individual level may or may not be capable of explaining who actually wins the election. Explaining election outcomes requires explaining changes in electoral behavior from one election to the next. Elections, in other words, must be viewed in dynamic terms.[1] This research focuses, therefore, on establishing in a systematic fashion the linkages between those forces which influence individual voters and the factors that explain the election outcome itself.

This work is specifically concerned with the impact of issues on electoral behavior. The importance of issues in explaining voting behavior has been perhaps the single most controversial aspect in the voting behavior research. I make the crucial and too fully neglected point that any discussion of the resonance of issues requires clarification of whether we are talking about individual-level voting behavior or election outcomes. Whether or not issues are influential at either level requires that a particular set of conditions be met. At the individual level, special attention is paid to the impact of issues unmediated by partisan linkages, as opposed to the influence of issues that are mediated by party. The essential finding here is that most issues are only capable of explaining voting behavior when they are linked or mediated by party or, more specifically, by the party viewed as best able to handle that particular issue. At the aggregate level, my primary concern is to look at those issues which explain outcomes. I show that only when issues are highly salient, exhibit strong linkages to a party, and are capable of explaining shifts over time from one election to the next, can we say with confidence that the issue was a determining factor in the election. The context of a particular election will determine whether or not those conditions are evident.

Several themes related to the issue-election outcome linkage are developed in this book. One is the question of the kinds of decision rules voters use in making electoral decisions. Do voters think in retrospective terms, or do they vote prospectively, considering the future consequences of choosing a particular party or candidate? Relatedly, we look at whether voters make decisions on the basis of a simple "reward-punishment" model of decision making, as opposed to an "issue-priority" model which requires voters to ascertain the issue priorities of the respective parties and understand the future consequences of supporting a particular party. I also introduce the notion of a "political debate" model of electoral support, which argues that whether or not issues work for or against a particular party or candidate results from the nature of the campaign dynamics in each particular election. Another theme relates to the question of whether voters respond on the basis of valence versus positional issues.[2] The findings to be presented here have significant implications for the debate over the role of valence versus positional issues and call into question some of the assumptions concerning valence issues and their effects. Also examined is the role that economic issues play in influencing voting behavior and outcomes. This work examines the influence of economic issues, specifically concern about inflation and unemployment, from the standpoint of both individual behavior and their ability to influence who wins and loses presidential elections. The role of economic issues is discussed within a broader context involving questions of retrospective versus prospective models of voting. Finally, the importance of issues is evaluated in terms of policy or election mandates. We are primarily concerned with discovering just what is a mandate, and under what conditions can one be said to exist. Elections are often viewed as representing a signal or approval from the electorate for certain policy related actions on the part of elected policymakers. This work contends that only rarely, if ever, do the conditions exist for such a sweeping interpretation.

The book is organized in a reasonably straightforward fashion. Chapter 2 expands on some of the general themes that have just been described and provides details of the kinds of models and analysis that are used in the analytic chapters. Chapters 3 through 6 discuss the presidential elections of 1972 through 1984. Each chapter begins with a general overview of the key events and dynamics of the campaign. Next, I look at influences on individual voting behavior in each election—i.e., which factors explain why individuals vote for the Republican or Democratic candidates. Bivariate tabular as well as multivariate analyses are presented. Finally, I present analyses of factors influential in explaining election outcomes. Chapter 7 recapitulates the findings and places them within a broader theoretical perspective. Lastly, Chapter 8 offers a brief overview of the 1988 election campaign within the context of the earlier discussion.

Two technical appendices are also included. Appendix A describes how the variables are constructed, and Appendix B describes the statistical technique of probit, which is used in the individual-level multivariate analyses.

2

Issues and
Presidential Elections

As Steven Rosenstone has recently noted, most political scientists working in the area of electoral behavior have been almost exclusively concerned with the determinants of individual-level voting behavior.[1] This is perhaps only natural, particularly given the fact that before the early 1950s large scale survey research was, for a number of reasons, impractical. Hence, prior to this time there had been an almost complete lack of systematic empirical knowledge concerning the behavior of individual voters. Although the past thirty years have witnessed an almost exponential increase in our knowledge and level of sophistication concerning the factors influencing individual-level voting behavior, both in terms of the statistical techniques used and the increasingly sophisticated models developed, political scientists have virtually ignored questions involving the dynamics and determinants of election outcomes.

Numerous multivariate analyses have demonstrated why, in a given election year, some voters support the Republican candidate for president while other voters support the Democratic candidate. What I am interested in explaining is why a political party and its presidential candidate may win one election but lose the next. The use of cross-sectional data involving discrete slices of time is by itself not sufficient to explain the dynamic processes that are involved in producing actual election outcomes. Cross-sectional studies focusing exclusively on the individual level simply do not provide us with sufficient information to allow statements concerning those factors which produce *changes* from one election to the next. As Rosenstone notes, there is a difference between determining what factors contribute to individual voting choice in a particular election or how many voters are affected by an issue, and determining whether those same factors actually contribute to shifts in voter allegiance from one election to the next. The purpose of this work is to evaluate the extent to which the determinants of individual voting behavior influence aggregate-level outcomes, with a particular focus on the influence of economic factors. To the extent that this work achieves that goal, it will contribute to a more general theory of elections.

Individual Voting Behavior

Since this work is aimed at explicating the relationship between individual behavior and aggregate outcomes, a brief review of the former is in order. This also allows for an opportunity to develop some themes that will be dealt with in the succeeding chapters.

Much of the current work in voting behavior has its origins in the "Michigan model" developed in the 1950s by Campbell and his associates at the University of Michigan.[2] Basically, they posited three basic attitudinal determinants of the vote. These were partisanship, candidate evaluations, and issues-attitudes. They later argued that partisanship, or partisan identification, functioned as the primary influence on voting behavior, as well as serving to shape both evaluations of candidates and issue orientations.[3] They suggested the existence of a "funnel of causality" model in which party identification, candidate attitudes and issues each has direct effects on voter choice, and party identification has indirect effects by its influence upon issues and candidate attitudes. The upshot of this was, however, that party identification was the single, overwhelmingly dominant factor influencing one's voting decisions. To attribute individual voting decisions to long-term, relatively unchanging psychological processes was a major blow to the traditional view of the classic democratic citizen. This view stressed politically knowledgeable individuals making voting decisions on the basis of rational, issue-based concerns rather than long-term psychological forces. Although their model allowed issues to play a potential role for individuals, they found, for instance, that significant percentages of those studied possessed virtually no issue awareness, that in most cases intensity of feelings about issues was often minimal, and that in many cases a majority were unable to recognize party differences on issues.[4]

Basically, these findings were suggestive of a relatively uninformed, unsophisticated electorate. Such conclusions were reinforced by other findings of the authors of *The American Voter* and the work of Philip Converse. This evidence had to do with the role of ideology and the presence of "nonattitudes" within the American electorate. By the early 1960s a new consensus had emerged that, to the extent citizens think about issues, most do so using immediate and concrete frames of reference. Rather than conceptualizing politics and issues in ideological, liberal-conservative terms, most voters structured the political world and issues in terms of "group benefits" and "the nature of the times."[5] In addition to the lack of any abstract conceptualization of politics, voters tended to exhibit little consistency, either over time or in the sense of maintaining an internally consistent position, on a set of issues at a particular point in time. Lastly, Converse has argued that the study of individual opinions on issues runs the risk of measuring attitudes and beliefs that are actually nonexistent. Individuals may feel compelled to give a response simply to avoid appearing foolish. Indeed, Converse has argued that many of the apparent responses to questions involving issue attitudes and positions are in fact not expressions of an actual belief but of a "nonattitude."[6]

It should be stressed that the apparent existence of a politically unsophisticated electorate is not taken to mean that citizens were stupid or irrational. Indeed, one could make the claim that voters were in fact acting rationally in an economic sense because the effort needed to obtain information on issues would be so costly and the payoff so minimal that to do so would be irrational.[7] Nonetheless, voters were now seen in a considerably less favorable light. By the 1970s the original "Michigan model" came under challenge. This occurred about the time that researchers began noticing an apparent decline in the importance of partisan affiliation within the electorate. If partisanship was declining as a long-term force, then it was plausible to assume that other forces might take on an increasingly influential role. Several researchers have suggested that evaluations of candidates have come to play such a role. Samuel Kirkpatrick, for instance, has shown that within the set of possible short-term forces, the influence of candidate images on the vote has steadily increased, being accompanied by a simultaneous decline in the relevance of party images.[8] Markus and Converse concluded that candidate personality had the strongest direct effect on the vote, even though partisan identification produced the strongest total effect.[9] Other researchers were able to substantially replicate those results. Among these studies, Kinder and Abelson's analysis of the 1980 election concluded that judgments of candidate competence and the intensity of positive and negative feelings engendered were more important factors than party identification, policy positions or assessments of national economic conditions.[10] With these findings as support, others have concluded that candidate evaluations are based primarily on how the candidate—if an incumbent—has performed in office or, in the case of the challenger, will perform in the future.[11] In one important sense, candidate assessments can become an indicator of performance evaluations by the electorate.[12]

Generally speaking, however, no real agreement exists on how to measure the electorate's evaluation of candidates. Although some researchers, such as Markus and Converse, have relied upon comparative feeling thermometer scores, others have used more specific measures of candidate evaluation. More importantly, from the standpoint of this study, there is a suggestion that thermometer scores may actually represent a "surrogate" for vote choice, in which case the inclusion of such variables would result in a highly mis-specified model.[13] Alternatively, less generalized measures such as competence may be highly correlated with thermometer scores or serve in some cases as surrogates for agreement on issue positions. In either case, the inclusion of such variables in a voting model could create difficulties.

Issues and Voting Behavior

The chief challenge to the Michigan model was the belief that issues are important in the voters' decision calculus. One of the early efforts to rescue the American voter from the obloquy to which he or she had apparently been consigned was that of V. O. Key, who argued that a significant subset of voters use a simple decision rule. According to Key, voters make voting decisions on the basis of a general assessment of the past performance of the party in power. If, on a set of salient issues, that assessment is positive, voters will tend to support that party. If the assessment is negative, they will support the opposition.[14] Unlike "pure" issue voting, such an approach precluded the need for voters to make judgments concerning partisan or candidate differences on issues. Anthony Downs's seminal theoretical contributions offered an even stronger critique of the early consensus.[15] Downs argued for the existence of a rational, utility maximizing electorate whose voting decisions were based on assessments of past party policy on salient issues and utilizing that information to project future performance. Morris Fiorina has suggested that voters use both retrospective and prospective evaluations in arriving at their vote decision.[16] Others have contended that voters use different decision rules depending upon whether candidates are incumbents or challengers.[17] Kuklinski and West also found evidence of prospective economic voting in U.S. Senate elections.[18] Others have uncovered evidence for the existence of "issue publics" whereby, on issues of concern to them, voters tend to be informed, aware of party differences, and prepared to vote on the basis of those differences.[19] Still another important "revisionist" work has suggested that while the Michigan researchers' original assumptions concerning the dominance of partisanship were true for the politically quiescent 1950s, the electorate had undergone a transformation resulting from ideological conflict and higher levels of education.[20] The ability of voters to respond to issues depends to a great extent on the willingness and ability of candidates and parties to articulate issue positions.[21] The degree of polarization between candidates and parties influences the perceptions of salience and party differentials at the mass level. An election characterized by significant differences between the candidates or parties should see a higher level of issue voting than an election in which candidate or party differences are muted. The extent to which voters include a prospective component in their decision making may be a function of specific electoral circumstances.

Reward-Punishment and Issue-Priority Voting

Voting on the basis of issues can be expressed, as already seen, in terms of a temporal dimension: retrospective or past-oriented versus prospective or future-oriented voting. Indeed, we can even assume a continuum, with pure retrospective and prospective voting anchoring the two extremes, while the Downsian-Fiorina approach—that voters use the past to make assessments of the future—occupies an intermediate position. There is a means of conceptualizing issue voting which draws upon insights of the previous approach. This can be described as reward-punishment versus issue-priority voting. Indeed, Key coined the former term to describe the voters' decision-making rule.[22] It assumes that voters make their electoral decisions based on their assessment of the government's performance on salient questions and issues. If the performance assessment is positive, then, all other factors being equal, the voters will reward the incumbent with their vote. Otherwise, they will punish the incumbents by voting for the opposition. In addition to the obvious fact that reward-punishment voting is retrospective in nature, it also relies solely upon the performance of the incumbents, and in its original form left no room for any kind of comparative assessment of parties or candidates.

In contrast to the reward-punishment model, the issue-priority model requires *prospective* judgments about the policy intentions and capabilities of the governing parties.[23] Although the assumption of a retrospectively oriented electorate has tended to dominate the voting and political support literature, we have already seen that there is a body of research which supports the notion of prospective thinking within the electorate. The issue-priority model assumes that voters perceive the parties to have different issue priorities. According to this model, voters offer or withdraw support based on the perceived priorities of competing parties. Voters would not necessarily punish a Republican administration for high or increasing price levels because they perceive that the Republicans are more concerned about and better able to deal with the problem.

In a similar fashion, voters would not necessarily offer or withdraw support from a Democratic administration during periods of high unemployment because they believe the Democrats are more concerned about unemployment and are better able to handle this problem. Such voter perceptions certainly do not have to be limited to economic issues, and could readily apply to other issues and conditions such as crime, aspects of foreign policy and so forth. All that is required is that voters (whether correctly or incorrectly) perceive that one party is better able to deal with the issue than another. There is evidence, however, that, at least in the economic domain, beliefs are grounded in objective macroeconomic circumstances. For example, Douglas Hibbs finds a difference of over 5 percent lower equilibrium levels for unemployment between Democratic and Republican presidents, with Democratic presidents being associated with lower unemployment. The downside of this is, of course, that given the "Phillips-Curve" tradeoff, the lower unemployment generates more inflation.[24] In contrast, Republican presidents are associated with higher unemployment resulting from efforts to maintain lower levels of inflation. It is assumed that the different parties reflect the concerns of the core coalitions of the respective parties. The Republican party consists disproportionately of more upscale voters who are somewhat more insulated from unemployment concerns but more worried by the impact of inflation. The Democratic constituency, representing a disproportionate number of lower and working class citizens, is more hard-hit by unemployment, hence their relative emphasis on jobs.

An alternative to both the reward-punishment and issue-priority models of voting behavior is the political debate approach.[25] It assumes that decisions made by voters in an election are in response to the context of the campaign and the persuasiveness of the parties and candidates in either highlighting issues favorable to them or in defusing potentially troublesome issues which might otherwise work to their disadvantage. The existence of a political debate model would be suggested by "flip-flopping" from reward-punishment to issue-priority voting, or vice versa.

Valence and Positional Issues

There is a different way of classifying and evaluating issues which is relevant for this study. One approach differentiates "hard" issues which require voters to make complex decisions over competing policy trade-offs, and "easy" issues which are concerned with ultimate policy ends and tend to be symbolic in nature, requiring less cognitive sophistication. In contrast to the latter, "hard" issues require a voter to possess a considerable amount of substantive information about issues and the positions of the candidates and parties. In this approach suggested by Carmines and Stimson, crime would be an example of an "easy" issue while Vietnam would be suggestive of a "hard" issue.[26] A similar conceptualization has been offered by Butler and Stokes who distinguish between "positional" and "valence" issues.[27] Positional issues are quite similar to "hard" issues in that they offer possibilities for a wide array of alternative candidate or party positions. Relatedly, they are issues in which debate tends to revolve around policy "means" rather than "ends." Valence issues, in contrast, are issues about which a consensus exists concerning the desirability or undesirability of some condition within the society and which are primarily concerned with ends rather than means.[28] In general, as noted by Butler and Stokes, valence issues should be more likely to have a more dramatic effect on voting decisions (and election outcomes), provided that a party can be linked, either positively or negatively, to a particular issue. This is because the cognitive requirements placed on the voter are substantially less. Voting on positional issues requires voters to perceive policy differences between the parties or candidates on often complex issues. No such burden is placed on the electorate when they are confronted with valence issues.

The valence-positional issue dichotomy is not without its critics. One influential argument is that all issues have positional characteristics.[29] Prosperity or depression is often cited as a classic example of a valence issue since prosperity is a universal "good" and depression a "bad." But while the ends of policy are accepted, this may not be the case for the means. A rational strategy for a party vulnerable on a valence issue could be to point out possible inconsistencies or weaknesses in the other party's position, or emphasize that the current incumbents can better deal with the problem. This is similar to the issue-priority model of electoral behavior and the kinds of party strategies thus engendered. It could, of course, also be consistent with a political debate model of voting behavior.

The presence of valence and positional issues in a political campaign (assuming a dichotomy) has direct implications for whether voters respond retroactively or proactively. If there is any issue which would seem amenable to retrospective voting, it should be a valence issue, since voters are responding to already existing conditions. To the extent that voters respond to positional issues, they of necessity are required to make decisions as to what parties will do in the future. Of course, this does not gainsay the likelihood that voters make these judgments, at least partially, on the basis of previous behavior of parties or candidates.

Economic Voting

As anyone only casually familiar with the work done in the area of voting behavior will attest, the literature is replete with both individual and aggregate-level analyses of the impact of economic conditions on voting behavior. The major themes of the work in this area can be described in terms of two dimensions. The first incorporates the question of whether voters make their decisions on the basis of egocentric, or "pocketbook," evaluations or sociotropic assessments of economic performance. Egocentric voting involves making voting decisions based on personal reasons or one's economic and financial standing. Sociotropic voting, in contrast, consists of voting decisions being based on assessments of national economic conditions. There is no definite answer as to which approach is utilized by voters. The "pocketbook" approach has tended to receive the most support in the literature, but recently Kinder and Kiewiet have found evidence that voters do indeed respond on the basis of national assessments of the economy.[30] Based on results obtained from U.S. congressional and presidential elections, they contended that judgments of collective economic performance play a more important role than personal economic and financial conditions.[31] It has also been suggested that voters can be arranged along a continuum ranging from egocentric voters at one extreme to sociotropic voters at the other.[32] Different groups within the electorate may make decisions based on different criteria, dependent on their levels of sophistication and levels of information an individual is capable of handling. Still other findings point to group membership being a salient reference point, serving as a bridge linking the two extremes.[33]

The second dimension has already been explored in the more general discussion of issue voting. This involves the question of whether voters use retrospective or prospective decision rules in making their voting decisions and, in a derivative sense, it can relate to the question of whether voters adopt reward-punishment or issue-priority approaches to making electoral choices. To summarize these findings, while most of the literature traditionally has supported the retrospective approach, more recent empirical examinations of this question have suggested the existence of prospective considerations impinging on electoral judgments. Several important findings have been obtained using both aggregate and survey results. Kramer, for instance, in his seminal article, suggested that the national vote share of the president's party in a given year is a function of macroeconomic conditions, particularly changes in real per capita income from the previous year.[34] Stigler, in a celebrated response to Kramer, argued that economic conditions have little, if any, effect on voting behavior.[35] Others, such as Arcelus and Meltzer, arrived at similar conclusions.[36] However, other aggregate analyses have tended to support Kramer's work. Tufte found that economic conditions, specifically personal disposable income, significantly influence the outcome of House elections.[37] Bloom and Price expanded on Kramer's original findings by asserting that the effects of economic conditions tend to be *asymmetrical* to the extent that unemployment and other factors hurt the party of the president, while favorable economic events do not necessarily produce a correspondingly favorable reaction from the electorate.[38]

One of the most recent and sophisticated models using aggregate data has been developed by Rosenstone. He found that changes in real personal disposable income can account for significant shifts in the behavior of the electorate from one election to the other.[39] Most aggregate studies of economic influences on voting assume a retrospectively oriented electorate, although some aggregate-level studies of presidential popularity have turned up evidence of prospective considerations at work in the electorate.[40]

Survey-level findings have supported both retrospective and prospective views of economic voting. Key provided the theoretical rationale for the former by suggesting voters simply evaluate how the economy has performed and reward or punish the incumbent on the basis of whether some threshold of performance has been obtained.[41] Kuklinski and West, already cited, found evidence for a prospective dimension. Lewis-Beck, in a study of Western European electorates, concluded that prospective elements of decision making were at least as important as past-oriented considerations,[42] and more recently has uncovered further evidence of such temporal features in the U.S.[43] Recent studies by Fiorina[44] and Kiewiet[45] provide evidence for both retrospective and prospective elements of thinking. Miller and Wattenberg, in a refinement of this theory, suggested that retrospective evaluations of the economy, as well as evaluations of other issue areas, are more likely to be applied to presidential incumbents. Challengers, however, are more likely to be evaluated prospectively. Most elections over the last two decades, then, have been significantly influenced by retrospective evaluations of incumbent performance.[46]

Taken together, the findings suggest that any effort to classify the electorate as being comprised of purely sociotropic or egocentric voters, or as retrospective or prospective, is too simplistic. Voters, in all likelihood, possess a complex mix of economic judgments and evaluations. Additionally, these evaluations, and the "mix," may change over time, depending on the political and economic context.[47]

Election Outcomes and Political Mandates

As noted at the outset, most research has dealt with the determinants of individual voting behavior rather than with explanations of election outcomes. And, to reiterate, the factors governing election outcomes may or may not relate to those forces that are important at the individual level. While this study differs in that it explores the linkages between individual behavior and outcomes, an examination of the prior research will clarify several points that I will make in this work.

One early study by Stokes indicated that Democrats' net strength in the 1960s had increased due to increasingly favorable perceptions of party positions on social welfare, social security and the like.[48] Time-series studies, just mentioned, that use aggregate data show that changes in real personal disposable income have a dramatic effect on congressional election outcomes.[49] Similar findings have been found for presidential elections. Ray Fair found that changes in real economic activity, whether measured as unemployment or per capita GNP, have equally strong effects on outcomes.[50] Gregory Markus' work helps illustrate a major concern of this book.[51] Markus found that changes in subjective personal financial status played an important role in explaining voting behavior, but could not explain the outcome of presidential elections between 1956 and 1984. Change in real personal disposable income, however, was important not only at the individual, but also at the aggregate level. Steven Rosenstone's findings, also mentioned earlier, substantially confirmed Markus' findings, and also concluded that certain social welfare and social issues have played an important role. Using a substantially different methodology, Stanley Kelley provides a comprehensive analysis for the 1964, 1972, and 1980 elections, concluding that candidate competence and social welfare issues were crucial to President Johnson's election victory, while competence and Vietnam substantially explained Richard Nixon's defeat of George McGovern.[52] Kelley, in fact, refers to 1972 as a "close" landslide in that the issues producing the landslide were nonpartisan in their implications, while issues relating to the New Deal remained salient and working in favor of the Democrats. And as for 1980, issues of the economy, as might be expected, appeared to play a crucial role.

In one of the most comprehensive comparative treatments of the subject, Budge and Farlie examine the causes of election outcomes in twenty-three Western democracies, including the United States.[53] They lend support to the "issue-priority" model of voting behavior in that the issue of inflation or unemployment produces net aggregate effects in favor of conservative parties, while issues of unemployment and social justice tend to be associated with more left-wing parties. Presumably, parties that "own" a particular issue will benefit in the election to the extent that the issue in question increases in salience. An important point they make, which needs to be stressed, is that while many issues may be salient and perhaps good predictors of voting behavior at the individual level, unless they affect a rather large subset of voters, their overall effect will be trivial. Issues must not only be salient among a large proportion of the electorate—they must also work preponderantly to the benefit of one party before they can influence the outcome. Not surprisingly, Budge and Farlie find that most issues produce relatively small net effects and these issue effects may not vary much from one election to the next, although the relatively centrist inclinations of the two parties, along with possible candidate effects, may make for a much more volatile situation. Budge and Farlie's findings suggest that issues that might work in classic valence fashion in some party systems—to the extent parties are punished for certain conditions prevailing under their incumbency—may operate in a somewhat different fashion in party systems where partisan differences are more clear. Issue volatility and the extent to which parties gain or lose on particular issues can also be crucial in determining the winners of the election contest. The mutability of issue-party linkages should make the election campaign and debate even more important in helping to decide the election outcome. In substantial part, according to Clarke et al., the turnover in government control in several countries in the 1970s, including the U.S., was largely due to changes in issue concerns from one election to the next, combined with changes in issue-party links.[54]

We are reminded that elections must be portrayed in dynamic terms. The mix of issues, candidates, and other short-term forces vary over time. Even the electorate is not a static entity, as older voters are replaced by younger age cohorts and as voters who participate in one election sit out the next, or vice versa. In one inquiry having significant application to my work, Clarke and his colleagues found substantial vote switching from one party to another from the 1974 to the 1979[55] and from the 1979 to the 1980 Canadian general elections,[56] as well as evidence of those individuals ("transients") who drop into and out of the electorate having the potential to influence election outcomes. The authors point out that election *outcomes* are determined by those forces which allow one party to hold supporters while simultaneously drawing new supporters either from those who "switch" their vote, from transients who reenter the electorate, or from those "new" voters entering the electorate for the first time. This is a recurring theme in my work.

Clarke et al. studies showed that, in the Canadian context at least, although there is considerable instability in *individual voting behavior*, this instability rarely translates into wide swings in *election outcomes*. Only occasionally, such as in the 1958 or 1984 federal elections, do short-term forces operate in a distinctly unidirectional fashion so as to significantly influence actual election outcomes. This is most likely to occur when a valence issue is present.

In the case of the 1984 election, Kornberg and Clarke have found that on economic, confederation, resource and a variety of social issues, the Conservatives were favored by overwhelming margins as the party closest on "most important issue." The Tories were favored by 53–14 percent over the Liberals on economic issues, which included the specific issues of unemployment, state of the economy, deficit, and inflation.[57]

To the extent that economic issues play a dominant role, these findings parallel in some respects those in this study for the American elections of 1976 and 1980. More specifically, the issue which would appear to be decisive in explaining the 1984 Canadian election outcome was unemployment, which was rated as "most important problem" by an impressive 31 percent of the electorate. Hence, the combination of *high saliency* plus unidirectional issue effects will produce major shifts in a party's electoral fortunes, which is of course what occurred in the 1984 Canadian general election when the Liberals were routed from power in a huge Tory landslide.

In the earlier 1974–79 federal election, economic issues and questions of majority government, at least to the extent that they were salient, tended to benefit the governing Liberals, whereas questions of wage and price controls provided a very marginal advantage to the Tories. But there was clearly no massive shift toward one party on any particular issue. With regard to 1979, economic issues worked to the benefit of the Tories, yet again the results could hardly be called decisive. There is no evidence the Tories obtained a mandate for change in any particular policy area. By 1980, the issues upon which the election was to be fought were considerably different from 1979. Still, most issues associated with the 1980 Canadian general election campaign had only limited impact, either because of lack of saliency or the absence of their favoring one party or another.

Any discussion of factors relevant to explaining election outcomes inevitably becomes entwined in the debate over election mandates. Successful presidential candidates like to claim that their victories represented a "mandate" to take certain actions. Nixon in 1972 and Reagan supporters in 1980 made extraordinary interpretations of their victories. To Kelley, mandates represent the belief that elections carry clear commands for future action by the government, and that this message is being sent by a clear majority of the electorate.[58]

A slightly different and perhaps more realistic interpretation is that a mandate exists whenever an issue can be shown to have a decisive effect on the outcome. Putting aside for the moment the question of how the effect is to be determined, issues that are decisive may not carry any policy directives. This is certainly the case if voters are simply responding to current conditions or otherwise voting on the basis of the government's past handling of a particular issue. This is clearly the case with valence issues where the electorate is merely responding to some condition within society. More discouraging, at least from the standpoint of those who believe elections are all about the future control of government policy, even issues in which voters respond with some element of concern for future consequences of government action will rarely convey sufficient information to constitute a command for particular policies or actions.

What kinds of issues and conditions may produce a policy mandate? It has been suggested that the nature of the party system may be important in encouraging issue debate and conflict, and in subsequently contributing to the ability of the electorate to make prospective choices.[59] Positional issues, which require a component of prospective thinking, might generate a mandate, but this could only occur when one party has a decisive advantage. This might occur, but only if one party allows itself to be perceived as distant from the median voter. Positional issues do not appear to be good candidates for generating decisive outcomes. Consequently, it is unlikely they can produce an election mandate. Valence issues, I contend, are more likely to produce decisive outcomes; however, they are typically seen as working in retrospective fashion, although the issue-priority model of behavior suggests there may indeed be a prospective element in voter responses to valence issues. Thus, one of the more intriguing questions this book hopes to answer is to what extent issues communicate citizen demands for specific courses of action by government.

A policy mandate, of course, is only one way in which citizens may exercise control over government. As Bingham Powell has noted, voters also exercise control through retrospective voter judgments. The "anticipation of future prospective voting encourages candidates to make commitments that will appeal to many voters. The threat of retrospective sanctions against those who betray their commitment encourages incumbents to keep their commitments."[60] A retrospective orientation to citizen control, nonetheless, provides a radically different view of democratic governance as compared to the mandate model.

If party differences and prospective voter orientations are crucial to the existence of mandates, what other factors would be consistent with the existence of policy mandates? Certainly two related considerations have already been addressed. To the extent that issue salience is volatile, and that the ability of parties to use many of those issues is uncertain, candidates and parties are placed in a much more ambiguous environment. But to the extent that certain issues remain on the political agenda, and that certain parties are seen as "owning" them, then the possibility for mandates should be enhanced, since parties would be less reluctant to offer policy commitments.

Individual Voting Behavior
and Election Outcomes

Although I have emphasized the critical difference between the determinants of individual voting behavior and factors influencing election outcomes, it is impossible to clarify the dynamics of the latter without first looking at the former. Factors that do not affect individual voting behavior cannot affect election outcomes. At the same time, factors having significant influence at the individual level may or may not have an effect at the macro, or aggregate, level.

Whether an issue actually influences election outcomes will depend on five factors. First, an issue must be salient to the individual elector. An issue that has no salience will be irrelevant to individual voting choice. Second, the issue must be linked to party. Individuals must be able to perceive one party as being able to deal more adequately with that issue than the other party. An issue may be salient, but unless a voter is able to identify a party as being preferred on that issue, it will not influence individual voting behavior.[61] Third, sufficient numbers of voters must identify the issue as important. Many issues arise in an election campaign. Only a few are likely to influence outcomes because only a handful are salient to a large number of voters. Fourth, the issue must work disproportionately in favor of one party. Last, the issue must be able to account for changes in support between the parties from one election to the next.

In order to explore the themes that were earlier described, a model is developed that allows for examination of individual and aggregated survey-level effects for the 1972 through the 1984 presidential elections. I have drawn on the University of Michigan's traditional pre-post national election studies for pertinent data. The analysis is conducted in two separate stages for the individual and aggregated levels. The individual-level component consists of a series of univariate, bivariate and multivariate analyses that rely on survey responses to the question, "What is the single most important problem facing the country?" This question, essentially retrospective in its orientation and tapping the sociotropic dimension, is then followed by, "Which party do you consider best able to handle [the problem]?" This question implies a prospective dimension and incorporates a performance assessment measure. In each election, the three to four most frequently cited problems are selected. Only those problems cited by five percent or more of the electorate were used. A major strength of the "most important problems" item is that they impose a minimum degree of constraint on the respondent. The chief weakness, of course, is the potential for allowing a voter to rationalize his reasons for supporting a particular party.

One quickly notes that the items used address the major *problem* facing the country. We must realize, however, that problems are not necessarily the same as issues. A problem may become an issue, but it does not necessarily *have* to be transformed into one. A problem becomes an issue only when it becomes a source of contention between the parties and candidates. A problem may be highly salient, but unless the parties and candidates "engage," it really has not been transformed into an issue. A problem can become an issue only after voters perceive one party as best able to deal successfully with it, or otherwise offer different policy solutions from which the electorate can choose.[62] Following univariate analyses, the relationship between issues and reported vote is explored.[63] In both bivariate and multivariate cases, the effect of issues alone, as well as the impact of issues when linked to party, is evaluated. In the multivariate case, I look at the impact of issues controlling for partisan identification. This provides a check on the more simple bivariate analyses, since rationalization and projection effects may exaggerate the influence of issues unless partisanship is controlled.[64] Details of variable construction and the technical details of the multivariate analytic techniques are described in appendices A and B. As in the bivariate case, two models are tested:

1. Repvote = Reppid + Dempid + Issue 1 + Issue 2 + . . . Issue N
2. Repvote = Reppid + Dempid + Issue-Party 1 + Issue-Party 2 + . . . Issue-Party N

In the first model Republican vote is related to partisan identification plus a set of issues drawn from the "most important problems" question. This unmediated model tests the impact of issues by themselves, controlling for partisanship. That is, no issue-party linkage has been specified. Issues can only have a statistically significant effect if the issue works preponderantly to the benefit of *one* party. Also, it will tell us those issues, if any, that are most likely to influence election outcomes, since only issues that work to the advantage of a single party can have such an effect.

The second (mediated) model simply tests for the impact of the issue-party linkages, controlling for partisanship. In other words, does the linkage of an issue to the party best able (in the voters' minds) to deal with it have an impact on voting, even controlling for partisanship? This gives issues a greater opportunity to demonstrate their importance, since we still want to know the extent to which those issues that do not benefit one party, but rather have cross-cutting effects, influence the vote. Special emphasis is placed on exploring economic issue effects in all models.[65]

The aggregate-level analyses (aggregated from the survey data) are concerned with the *dynamic* elements of elections. This is done first of all by simply looking at the structure of the electorate. The NES studies include questions which allow me to break the electorate down into a series of categories: those who have voted in the last and current elections, new voters, transients who vote in an election but not in another, and nonvoters. Turnover tables provide evidence of shifts in support from one party to another over the course of two elections.[66] The aggregate effects of issues are explored through a partitioning of the electorate into three categories: those who vote for the same party from one election to the next, those who switch, and those who are new to the electoral process, as well as those who failed to vote in the previous election but did vote in the current election. The net effects of issues can then be ascertained by calculating the percentage of those citing an issue as "most important" and examining the differential between those voting for the Republican versus Democratic nominee.

3

The 1972 Election:
Do Landslides Produce Mandates?

In 1972 President Richard Nixon won a landslide victory over his Democratic opponent George McGovern. The Nixon landslide was also surprising in that virtually none of the political pundits or polls had even hinted at the ultimate size of the Nixon victory. Prior to 1972, there were strong suggestions that Nixon was vulnerable to a Democratic challenge. The nation remained militarily involved in Southeast Asia, although the troop levels were being gradually reduced under Nixon's "Vietnamization" plan. Still, critics on and off the campuses contended that the war was not being ended quickly enough, and surveys suggested an increasing disillusionment with America's involvement in this unpopular war. The Kent State shootings in May of 1970, following the Cambodian incursion, served to reinforce the polarization that was taking place. Democrats who had been somewhat muted in their criticism became more vociferous in their opposition to Nixon administration policies.

In addition to the preeminent issue of Vietnam, the continued sluggishness of the nation's economy as well as the rate of inflation, high by post-war standards, continued to plague the president. By July of 1971 Nixon's approval rating had declined to a somewhat shaky 50 percent.[1] The Gallup Poll trend in Mr. Nixon's popularity over his first term is shown in Figure 3.1.[2] Unemployment and inflation data are given in Figure 3.2.[3] In August of 1971 Nixon responded to the economic crises with the imposition of wage and price controls and the removal of the U.S. from the gold standard. The same month Nixon announced the return of Henry Kissinger from a secret trip to Peking to discuss the normalization of relations between the United States and the People's Republic of China. These events help illustrate the ability of a president to enhance his chances for reelection.

Nonetheless, there was no shortage of Democratic challengers to Nixon. Senators Edmund Muskie and Hubert Humphrey both planned to enter the primaries. Other lesser-known figures included George

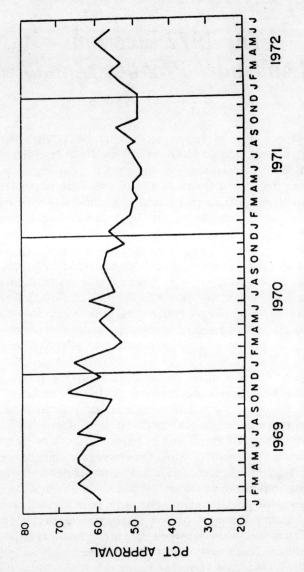

Figure 3.1.   Trend in Nixon Gallup Approval Rating, 1969-1972

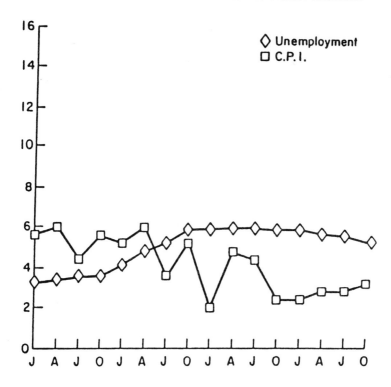

Figure 3.2.   Trends in Inflation and Unemployment,
1969-1972

McGovern, who would base much of his campaign on his opposition
to the Vietnam war, and John Lindsay, the former Republican and now
Democratic mayor of New York. And, of course, George Wallace, the
segregationist governor of Alabama, was making another bid for the
nomination with appeals similar in nature to his fiery law and order
campaign of 1968.

One Gallup survey taken in January of 1972 showed the GOP trailing
the Democratic party by ten points as the party best able to deal with
the nation's most important problems. However, this was an improvement
over the 18 point gap that had favored the Democrats in August. Still,
this same poll did suggest a moderate sense of optimism about the
coming year, of which an incumbent administration might be able to
take advantage.[4]

The presidential race was in full swing by early 1972, with most
predicting a Muskie nomination victory. One Gallup survey taken in

February of 1972 showed Nixon in a statistical deadheat with the Maine senator, holding only a 43–42 percent lead, with 10 percent supporting former Alabama Governor George C. Wallace. Wallace, the segregationist, was essentially picking up where he left off in 1968.[5]

Most of the assumptions concerning a close race had been premised upon the Democrats nominating a centrist who could hold together the old New Deal coalition. The consensus was that Muskie, the candidate of the Old Guard of the party, was the overwhelming favorite for the nomination. Senator George McGovern, who had announced his candidacy in January of 1971, appeared to have made hardly a dent in terms of name recognition. His national support in one Gallup survey hovered at a miniscule 3 percent. Muskie, however, fell victim to the expectations which had been created by his own campaign and the news media. Although Muskie went on to win the New Hampshire primary with 48 percent of the vote to McGovern's 37 percent, this outcome was far below the expected 60 to 65 percent Muskie vote which had been suggested by some.[6]

Muskie's problems tended to illustrate the difficulties of front-runner status, being a centrist within the Democratic party and being seen as a mainstream liberal. Muskie appeared unable to attract truly committed supporters to his candidacy. His inability may have resulted from the fact that relatively few voters seemed to know Muskie's issue positions. The deficiency might not be a problem in a general election. Indeed, it might prove beneficial, but it could prove damaging in primary contests in which the participants tend disproportionately to be party activists.

In succeeding primaries, McGovern continued to exceed expectations, winning the Wisconsin and Nebraska primaries in early May. Muskie, forced out of the nomination race following the Wisconsin primary, was replaced by Senator and former Vice-President Hubert Humphrey as the mainstream Democratic candidate. The California primary of June 6, however, in which McGovern edged Humphrey by 46 to 41 percent, essentially sealed the nomination victory. McGovern won his party's nomination through a variety of circumstances. The more traditional leadership of the party, represented by figures such as Humphrey, Muskie and Senator Henry Jackson, had been partially discredited by their tardy opposition to the Vietnam war, an opposition which McGovern had made the centerpiece of his campaign. Also, by adopting a distinctive set of positions on Vietnam, defense, and a variety of other social issues, he was able to distinguish himself from the rest of the primary field. However, the very necessity of taking distinct positions on issues in order to attract activist and primary support would provide convenient targets not only for centrist Democrats such as Humphrey and Jackson, but also for Nixon in the general election campaign.

Although beaten by McGovern, the other candidates seemed to make little effort at reconciliation. This was also true of the traditional powerbrokers in the party such as organized labor and Mayor Daley. Humphrey, who had really begun to hammer on the theme of McGovern's radicalism during the California primary, refused to bow out of the race. At the convention the McGovern forces won the convention battles over allocating delegates in the California primary and the seating of the Chicago delegates under the leadership of Chicago mayor Richard Daley. These battles which played themselves out at the convention seemed to exacerbate the wounds already suffered by the party. Although the conflicts at the convention were mild compared to the chaos of the 1968 convention, the animosities developed during the campaign and reflected during the convention clearly did not help.

As if McGovern was not beginning the campaign with sufficient handicaps, the candidate was forced to replace his original vice-presidential running mate, Senator Thomas Eagleton. The latter was forced to leave the ticket when the media began reporting that he had been hospitalized for nervous exhaustion on at least three occasions, with electro-shock therapy being administered twice. McGovern, who had spent much of the year spelling out in considerable detail his positions on issues such as Vietnam, defense, civil rights and others, was now confronted with questions relating to his and Eagleton's competence. The replacement of Eagleton with Sargent Shriver, a Kennedy in-law and former director of the Office of Economic Opportunity (OEO), finally ended the drama, but questions continued to be raised about McGovern's credibility following this public relations disaster.

McGovern was facing a unified Republican party and an increasingly strong President Nixon, who had achieved two major foreign policy triumphs within the last year.[7] A Gallup survey conducted just after the President's trip to Peking in February showed a 56 percent approval rating, a statistically significant 7 point gain from a similar survey taken in early January.[8] Nixon's orchestration of foreign policy spectaculars seemed to be a rather potent reminder to the Democratic hopefuls that the President, merely by virtue of his position, is in an ideal position to dominate the media and generate favorable publicity. Thus, voters were forced to contrast the President, *being President* and appearing to "take charge," with a bevy of Democratic candidates who moved around the country merely proclaiming what they would do in the future if elected.

Following the Nixon trip to the Soviet Union in June, which produced the signing of the first Strategic Arms Limitation (SALT 1) agreement, his approval rating was at an all-time high of 60 percent.[9] The gradual withdrawal from Vietnam and the apparent reconciliation with the Soviet

Union and China appeared to be working. Unemployment was declining; there is evidence that, in this regard, the Nixon administration was following a classical political business cycle strategy of increasing government expenditures in an effort to reduce unemployment prior to the election.[10] In addition to these issues, earlier surveys had suggested that a major "sleeper" issue of the campaign was fear of crime. An April survey had shown that worry about crime and lawlessness, including drug abuse and what was perceived as a deterioration of moral values, was second only to Vietnam and the economy in importance as issues.[11] Nixon, given his previously forceful positions on crime, seemed much better placed to benefit from these concerns than the liberal George McGovern.

Clearly, Nixon seemed interested in obtaining backing from former supporters of George Wallace, to whom "law and order" appeals had proven so effective during the 1968 campaign. Indeed, Nixon may well have benefitted from the forced withdrawal of Governor Wallace from the presidential race following his near fatal shooting during the Maryland Democratic primary. The one major potential issue that failed to surface during the campaign was the Watergate break-in. In spite of the evidence linking the burglars to the Nixon reelection effort, McGovern's efforts to raise the visibility of the issue were to no avail.

By September of 1972, Nixon had virtually locked up the election. Most surveys, including Gallup, had Nixon leading by 20 points or more. The Gallup survey showed Nixon defeating McGovern 61 percent to 39 percent.[12] The remaining weeks of the campaign were anti-climactic. McGovern's efforts to highlight differences with Nixon on Vietnam and the economy were not successful. Nixon, conducting a "Rose Garden" strategy, simply ignored McGovern's sniping. McGovern's criticisms of Nixon's Vietnam policy may also have seemed a case of "sour grapes," particularly given the Administration's hints of a coming breakthrough with the North Vietnamese at the Paris Peace Talks. It became increasingly clear as the election approached that voters had no intention of rejecting Nixon's bid for reelection. The only real question left to be answered on election day was the size of the Nixon victory margin.

Although the issues appeared to work in favor of Richard Nixon in 1972, there is evidence that the magnitude of McGovern's defeat—if not the defeat itself—was attributable to the perception of the candidate as "dangerous." And as mentioned earlier, while the issues may have worked to the benefit of Nixon, these benefits were not readily transferable to other members of his party. In sum, the size of Nixon's triumph was in some sense fortuitous, depending upon a weak Democratic candidate and a cluster of issues of which Mr. Nixon was in position to take full advantage. In short, 1972 appeared to be an election in which the short-term forces were all working to assist the Republican presidential candidate.

Individual Voting Behavior in 1972

The previous section has served to outline the major dynamics of the 1972 presidential campaign and the chief issues which confronted the nation and candidates. In this section we turn to an explanation of issue effects on voting behavior in the 1972 presidential election.

Before looking at actual voting behavior, it will be useful to evaluate the kinds of issues salient to the electorate in 1972. Table 3.1 shows the responses to the "most important problems" question facing the country. Just over 25 percent cited Vietnam, followed by crime-disorder and inflation at approximately 20 and 13 percent, respectively. Among only those mentioning a problem, Vietnam was cited by approximately 26 percent of interviewees, while crime-disorder and inflation were mentioned by 21 and 14 percent, respectively. Herbert Asher has conducted a similar examination for recent elections.[13]

I should note there is one small difference between the 1972 analysis and subsequent years. When respondents are asked the "single most important problem" facing the country, it includes only those giving more than one answer. The results in this chapter are consequently based only on this subset of individuals. However, 84 percent of respondents did indeed cite more than one problem. This analysis also allows a comparison of issue-voting over the four elections, since the electoral behavior of those citing more than one issue may be more highly influenced by issues than others.

Each of these issues represented relatively long term problems facing the electorate. Both Vietnam and crime-disorder had also been rated as significant problem areas four years earlier in 1968, although inflation did not appear among the five most frequently cited problems. One stark difference between 1972 and 1968, however, was the dramatic decline of Vietnam as a salient issue. Whereas 43 percent of those citing a problem had mentioned this issue in 1968, a 17 point decline on this issue was observed for 1972. It would seem likely that this worked to the benefit of the incumbent administration in the latter year, even though the U.S. remained militarily involved. Nixon, it seems, had been at least partially successful in reducing the salience of Vietnam as an issue.

The question of crime and disorder was in part a carryover from the late 1960s. George Wallace had focused much of his campaign on the crime issue in 1968, with the argument that the courts and other permissive elements in society had contributed to a breakdown of "law and order."

TABLE 3.1 MOST IMPORTANT ISSUES IN 1972

Issue	N	Percentage Mentioning Problem as "Most Important"*	
		(1)	(2)
Vietnam	209	25.1	25.8
**Crime	170	20.2	20.6
Inflation	115	13.4	14.0

N is the number of respondents.

*(1) includes all respondents whether or not they cited a problem as most important. (2) includes only those mentioning a problem. However, see text for fuller explanation of this particular case.

**Crime consists of responses not only to crime but also to public disorder and drug usage.

TABLE 3.2 PARTY PREFERRED IN 1972 ON MOST IMPORTANT ISSUES*

Issue	Republican N %	Undecided N %	Democrat N %
Vietnam	80 (38.3)	86 (41.1)	43 (20.5)
Crime	39 (22.9)	109 (64.1)	22 (13.0)
Inflation	33 (28.7)	57 (49.5)	25 (21.7)

*N in each category is the number of respondents citing the party as best able to handle that particular issue. Numbers in parentheses are the percentages favoring that party on a particular issue.

What is difficult to measure, of course, is the extent to which the crime issue also tapped latent racial concerns within the American electorate which, in fact, may have served as a kind of surrogate for the more explicitly racial concerns of the 1960s.

Inflation, the issue which had not appeared in 1968, reflected the deteriorating state of the American economy resulting from deficit spending to finance Vietnam and the Great Society. But as we will see in succeeding chapters, the inflation issue had only begun to assert itself and to create problems for those aspiring to the presidency or those seeking to remain in the White House.

Among these issues, inflation and crime fit most closely the "valence" designation, while Vietnam would appear more a "positional" issue. A major concern of the analysis is the determination of the extent to which valence-type issues influence electoral behavior and what this tells us about partisan competition and the ability of elites to use issues to their advantage. At the same time, though, it is clear that the likelihood of any given issue having an impact on the election itself is small, given the relatively low salience of any given issue. It would have to work dramatically in favor of one party to have a chance of seriously influencing the outcome.

Table 3.2 serves to clarify these points. Here, respondents who have identified a particular problem are asked to identify the party best able to handle the issue. Clearly, across all issues a relatively large percentage of those identifying a problem as "most important" are undecided as to which party is most competent. However, for those who are capable of choosing between Democrats and Republicans, the Republicans are favored consistently over the Democrats, although the advantages are not dramatic.

With regard to Vietnam, the single most frequently mentioned issue, 38 percent of those who identified Vietnam as the single most important problem facing the nation said the Republicans offered the best solution. By contrast, only 21 percent favored the Democratic approach, while a plurality of 41 percent could or would not choose between the parties.

For both the crime and inflation issues, either a plurality or majority was unable to select a party they preferred on the issue. For crime, 23 percent favored the Republicans, suggesting that the Nixon hard-line positions on crime had produced some effect. Voters probably were not attributing the positions of George McGovern to the party as a whole.

Concerning inflation, Republicans again were narrowly favored, although 49 percent were unable to decide between the parties. As the reader will note, however, questions are phrased in terms of *party* rather than *candidate* preference. One could expect that any question relating to candidate preference might have provided a more clear cut set of responses in favor of the Republican candidate. This would almost certainly have been the case in 1972 when voters were offered the clearest set of choices since the 1964 Goldwater-Johnson campaign. Indeed, a Gallup survey conducted in October, just prior to the election, showed Nixon favored over McGovern by very healthy margins on most issues: 58–26 percent on Vietnam; 46–32 percent on inflation; and 50–25 percent on crime and lawlessness.[14]

These figures provide the first real hint as to the influence these issues may have had on the election outcome in 1972. None of the issues would appear to demonstrate either the necessary degree of salience, in the sense of being a major concern to a substantial portion of the electorate (with the possible exception of Vietnam), or their being linked favorably to a particular party. Only if one or more issues were clearly linked with one party could we anticipate major effects on the election's outcome. What is also of interest is that the two apparent valence issues—inflation and crime—do not appear to work against the incumbent's administration. The electorate does not simply react against the incumbents for the existence of these conditions; it either recognizes the inability of either party to handle the issue, or views the opposition as doing a worse job.[15] Hence, these initial findings are at least suggestive of an issue-priority effect at work.

The question of actual behavior, as opposed to attitudes, has not yet been addressed. What was the association between issues and individual electoral choice? Table 3.3 provides a simple bivariate analysis of reported vote in 1972. Among those citing Vietnam as most important, two-thirds or 67 percent supported Nixon and the Republicans. Among those who did not cite a particular problem, 64 percent reported having voted for Mr. Nixon. Virtually identical results are obtained when we examine the relationship between reported vote and inflation and crime, respectively. So, the argument that issues *by themselves* influence voting in a significant fashion is problematic, at least as regards the results of the bivariate analysis. Those who *cite* a problem are only marginally more likely to support the Republicans than those who do not. More important, the apparent lack of dramatic individual-level effects almost assures that none of these issues will have massive effects on the election outcome.

The picture changes dramatically when we examine the results of the data in Table 3.4. Here we have the relationship between vote and party best able to handle the particular problem. In each case the issue-party competence link produces overwhelming support for that particular party, whether Republican or Democrat. With regard to the most often cited problem, Vietnam, 89 percent of those viewing the Republicans as most competent voted for Mr. Nixon, whereas 79 percent who viewed the

TABLE 3.3   REPORTED PERCENTAGE VOTE FOR CANDIDATES IN 1972
BY SELECTED MOST IMPORTANT ISSUES

Candidate	Vietnam		Crime		Inflation	
	NM	M	NM	M	NM	M
McGovern	36.0	33.1	36.1	31.5	35.9	32.9
Nixon	64.0	66.9	63.9	68.5	64.1	67.1
(Total N=1,559)	1,408.0	151.0	1,435.0	124.0	1,480.0	79.0

- NM refers to those respondents <u>not mentioning</u> a problem as most important.

- M refers to those respondents <u>mentioning</u> a particular issue as most important.

NOTE: Percentages have been rounded to the nearest one-tenth percent.

Democrats as most competent supported McGovern. Similar results obtain for inflation and crime. The *differentials* in electoral support for the respective candidates by respondents citing a problem, as opposed to those capable of identifying a party as competent to handle it, is quite large in virtually every instance. These results clearly show that at the bivariate level of analysis, *issues*, when linked to *party*, are highly significant predictors of *individual* voting choice. But these findings have dampened any hope of finding a particular issue which has major effects at the aggregate level.

While these data can offer us some insight into the dynamics of an election, they cannot tell the whole story. This is because voter rationalization and projection effects may tend to distort possible issue effects. A more sophisticated approach is to conduct a multivariate analysis of the vote in which we evaluate the effects of various explanatory variables, controlling for all other variables in the analysis. Probit analysis was used to estimate the separate effects of partisanship and issues. In the first analysis presented in Table 3.5, the influence of issues *alone* (unmediated by party), along with the effects of partisan identification, are examined. The results (Model One) show that the unmediated impact of issues has relatively little influence on one's voting decision and explain very little beyond that already accounted for by partisanship. Interestingly, crime and disorder produce the strongest effect among the issues, but the effect is not statistically significant. Partisanship is overwhelmingly dominant, suppressing possible issue effects. Crime-

TABLE 3.4 PARTY PREFERRED ON MOST IMPORTANT ISSUES IN 1972
AND PERCENTAGE VOTE FOR CANDIDATES

	Party Preferred		
Issue	Republican %	Undecided* %	Democrat %
Vietnam			
McGovern	10.9	35.7	79.4
Nixon	89.1	64.3	20.6
N	64.0	1,461.0	34.0
Crime			
McGovern	9.1	35.8	73.7
Nixon	90.9	64.2	26.3
N	33.0	1,507.0	19.0
Inflation			
McGovern	--**	35.7	80.0
Nixon	100.0	64.3	20.0
N	26.0	1,513.0	20.0

(Total N = 1,559)

*The "undecided" category includes those who did not mention
a problem, since we assume that those undecided between the
Republican and Democratic parties on an issue behave no
differently than those not citing a problem.

** refers to no cases in cells

disorder is followed by inflation and Vietnam, respectively, in terms of
influencing the probability of voting Republican. Given the insignificance
of the inflation variable, few conclusions can be drawn concerning the
relative merits of the reward-punishment or issue-priority models, although the positive sign provides very tentative evidence of an issue-
priority effect. A similar conclusion, albeit a tentative one, can be drawn
concerning the issue of crime.

It is a different story when one looks at the second model which
examines the effects of issues mediated by party. Even when partisanship
is controlled, preference for the Republicans on an issue significantly
increases the probability of voting Republican. The manner in which
the issue variables were constructed dictates that all signs be positive.
All the issues become significant determinants of voter choice, over and
above the variance accounted for by partisanship alone. Vietnam produces

TABLE 3.5 PROBIT ESTIMATES OF EFFECTS OF PARTISANSHIP AND ISSUE-PRIORITY VARIABLES ON 1972 VOTE

Variables	Model One	Model Two
Constant	0.414/(0.065)*	0.429/(0.063)*
Republican Party ID	1.163/(0.117)*	1.120/(0.119)*
Democratic Party ID	-0.653/(0.081)*	-0.616/(0.082)*
Vietnam	0.094/(0.123)	0.836/(0.173)*
Inflation	0.156/(0.167)	1.131/(0.290)*
Crime	0.150/(0.137)	0.805/(0.240)*
N = 1456		
Estimated R^2	.36	.41
R^2 increment**	.01	.06
Rho	.40	.43
% correctly classified	.71	.73

*$P \leq$ .05

**R^2 increment refers to additional variance explained by the issue variables over and beyond that explained by partisanship alone.

a slightly larger coefficient than the others, although all are significant at the .05 level. Just as important, issues when linked to party add a relatively healthy 6 percent to the variance explained. These findings demonstrate the relevance of prospective assessments of performance in voters' decision making.

What all the analyses have suggested to date, however, is that no *single* issue generated the kind of unidirectional partisan shift in electoral support that would have produced a dramatic change at the aggregate level. To examine this more closely, though, a discussion of the 1972 election *outcome* is in order.

Individual Voting
and the 1972 Election Outcome

In the preceding section the influences which help determine the behavior of individual voters in elections were examined. We now turn to an examination of those factors which influence aggregate or macro-level outcomes. Before considering the specific influences on election outcomes, it is desirable to get an idea as to the dynamic and fluid nature of the electorate. An electorate is not a static entity. This is true for two reasons. First, voters may change their voting behavior from one election to the next. The idea of conversion has played a major role in works by Walter Burnham, who suggests this process is crucial to understanding critical realignments.[16] Others maintain their support for the same party. At the same time, the electorate itself is constantly changing through patterns of replacement. Although replacement is often thought of as a long term process through which older generations of voters are succeeded by younger generations, it can also occur in a more short-term sense, as some voters, for a variety of reasons, vote in some elections then fail to vote at other times. This reflects what Campbell has referred to as "peripheral" voters as opposed to the "core" voters who participate in a consistent manner.[17] To a great extent, the characteristics of the electorate in any specific election are largely a question of how many of the less interested voters are stimulated to vote.

Table 3.6 shows the sources of change in the electorate for 1972. This figure provides percentages based upon all members of the *eligible* electorate. This is important because it gives us some idea about the dynamic nature of the electorate. Forty-two percent of the total electorate in 1972 voted for the same party in both the 1968 and 1972 elections. But 15.7 percent of the electorate changed their vote between 1968 and 1972, either switching between the major party candidates over this period, or switching from Wallace in 1968 to a major party candidate in 1972. About 6.5 percent of the electorate is represented by transients who had been eligible but failed to vote in 1968. Finally, 28 percent of those eligible to vote in 1972 reported not voting. Of this total, about 13 percent were transient nonvoters who had voted in the previous election. The remainder were eligible to vote for the first time but failed to do so, or were consistent non-participants eligible to vote in both elections. As will be shown later, the relative impact of switchers, transients, abstainers and new voters can vary from one election to the next.

An examination of the "turnover" table (Table 3.7) provides a much better indication of the *direction* in which key groups in the electorate move from one election to another. The turnover table is set up simply by cross-tabulating reported voter behavior in 1968 with behavior in 1972. As the table shows, the pattern heavily favored Mr. Nixon and the Republicans. This is suggested first from looking at the percentages. A full 27.0 percent of Humphrey voters supported Richard Nixon in his reelection bid. Furthermore, the overwhelming percentage of Wallace

TABLE 3.6 SOURCES OF PERCENT CHANGE IN THE
1968-1972 ELECTIONS

Category	Electorate
Remain[1]	41.9%
Switchers (Major Party)[2]	9.9%
Switchers (Wallace to Major)	5.8%
Transients[3]	6.5%
New Voters[4]	8.1%
Transient and Newly Eligible Nonvoters[5]	12.8%
Nonvoters[6]	15.0%
(Total N = 2,145)	100.0%

[1]Those voting for same party in both 1968 and 1972.

[2]Those who switch from one party candidate to another between 1968 and 1972.

[3]Those voting in 1972 who were eligible to vote in 1968 but abstained.

[4]Those voting in 1972 who were ineligible to vote in 1968.

[5]Those eligible to vote in 1972 who voted in 1968 but abstained, and those newly eligible who failed to vote.

[6]Those who failed to vote in both 1968 and 1972.

TABLE 3.7 TURNOVER TABLE, 1968-1972 (1972 VOTING PATTERNS BY 1968 VOTING PATTERNS)

1972 Vote	1968 Vote				
	Nixon	Humphrey	Wallace	Non-Voter	Ineligible
Nixon	80.0	27.5	66.2	16.4	30.5
McGovern	9.9	58.7	17.6	14.0	31.2
Abstained	10.1	13.8	16.2	69.5	38.5
(Total N = 2,145)	750.0	509.0	148.0	463.0	275.0

chi-square = 1087.5, d.f. = 8, p < .001

Cramer's V = .50

supporters moved into the Republican column in 1972. A healthy 66 percent of Wallace voters opted for the Republican ticket in 1972, while only 18 percent supported George McGovern. Eighty percent of Nixon voters in 1968 reported staying with Nixon and the Republicans in 1972, while only 59 percent of those supporting Humphrey in 1968 also acknowledged voting for McGovern four years later. Hence, a 21 point "party loyalty" gap existed in favor of the Republicans.

One might surmise that the Wallace supporters of 1968 were attracted by the perceived proximity of Nixon on several issues, including Vietnam and the issue of crime and disorder. Overall, Mr. Nixon won out among the "switchers" by approximately 70–30 percent. So, while the switchers cannot claim to have provided the margin of victory, since their numbers in the electorate were relatively small, they certainly added a very comfortable margin to Mr. Nixon's victory totals. The behavior of the transients who moved back into the electorate in 1972, and of the new voters, is theoretically less interesting. Only 30 percent of those who were eligible to vote in 1968, but did not do so, actually voted in 1972. Of those who did vote, Mr. Nixon won out by a relatively narrow percent margin. The 1972 election does not appear to have significantly mobilized this quiescent group of citizens or prompted those who did reenter the process to move in any particular direction. Finally, among those entering the electorate for the first time, the two-party split was nearly even. There is certainly no evidence here of any massive youth movement working in favor of the Democratic candidate.

All of the above still begs the question of what may have precipitated these various movements within the electorate. In the following pages an effort will be made to shed light on these questions.

Issues and the 1972 Election Outcome

Table 3.8 is an effort to examine precisely the question of what might influence an election outcome. This table indicates the voting patterns for our different voter classifications in the 1972 election. For each issue, voters are identified as to whether or not they switched from one party to another since the last election, voted for the same party in successive elections, or are either entering the electorate for the first time or reentering the electorate after abstaining in the previous election.[18]

The analysis clearly shows that, on each of the issues, Mr. Nixon was preferred over Senator McGovern. For example, of those who switched to the Republican party from the Democrats, massive majorities favored the Republican party position on the three most important identified issues. For those who switched from one party to another and identified Vietnam, crime-disorder and inflation as most important, between 83

TABLE 3.8   EFFECT OF ISSUES IN THE 1972 PRESIDENTIAL
ELECTION*

| | 1972 Vote | |
Voting Pattern	Nixon	McGovern
Vietnam		
Switch (N = 338)	83 (1.5)	17 (0.3)
Remain (N = 899)	67 (3.5)	33 (1.7)
Enter/Reenter (N = 311)	<u>52 (1.0)</u>	<u>48 (0.9)</u>
	6.0	2.9
Crime		
Switch (N = 338)	86 (1.2)	14 (0.2)
Remain (N = 899)	68 (3.2)	32 (1.5)
Enter/Reenter (N = 311)	<u>56 (1.0)</u>	<u>44 (0.8)</u>
	5.4	2.5
Inflation		
Switch (N = 338)	85 (0.6)	15 (0.1)
Remain (N = 899)	70 (1.9)	30 (0.9)
Enter/Reenter (N = 311)	<u>54 (0.7)</u>	<u>46 (0.6)</u>
	3.2	1.6

(Total N = 1,548)

*Figures not in parentheses represent percentage support for candidate; figures in parentheses are vote as percentage of entire electorate.

and 86 percent moved to the Republican candidate, Mr. Nixon. For those either entering or reentering the electorate, Mr. Nixon and the Republicans are again favored, although as Table 3.9 clearly shows, the margins are much smaller. For instance, Mr. Nixon carried 52 percent of those mentioning Vietnam, 56 percent of those mentioning crime and 54 percent of those mentioning inflation.

As for the single largest voting bloc, i.e., those who voted for the same party in both 1968 and 1972, the advantage again goes to Mr. Nixon. Between 67 and 70 percent of those who remained with the same party supported the President, with his biggest advantage accruing on the issue of inflation. These percentages, however, can be misleading. Simply because one candidate has a massive advantage over his opponent on a particular issue does *not* mean that issue will have an impact on the election outcome. To influence the outcome an issue would have to be both highly salient *and* work to the advantage of one party.

On all issues combined, Mr. Nixon was favored by a net margin of about 7.5 percent, though no *single* issue appears to have had a dramatic effect on the vote. When we look at the influence of switching, where Mr. Nixon had huge advantages over Mr. McGovern in terms of sheer percentages on an issue, the influence on the actual election is fairly modest. The largest advantage was on Vietnam which produced a 1.2 percent net gain for the President. Mr. Nixon also attained a net gain of 1.8 percent among those who voted for the same party between 1968 and 1972. With regard to crime, Mr. Nixon obtained a net overall advantage of nearly 3 percent, with virtually all of the gain coming from switchers (1.0 percent) and loyalists (1.7 percent). Finally, on the inflation issue the President won an overall advantage of 1.6 percent, holding a net advantage of .5 percent among switchers and 1.0 percent among loyalists. In essence, no single issue so dominated the election as to clearly produce the outcome which has been discussed. Indeed, even if the advantages on the issues had been *reversed*, Mr. Nixon would have triumphed, albeit by a considerably smaller margin. On the basis of these findings, there is no evidence whatever that the 1972 election represented any kind of mandate for action by the just reelected Nixon Administration.

A possible problem with the previous analysis is that one is only examining the relationship between *concern* for an issue and electoral behavior. However, to parallel the individual-level analysis, the relationship between voting behavior and party preference on an issue is also examined. Table 3.9 produces results which, in the main, are not especially different from those just discussed. What is most important for our purposes is that the general *direction* of partisan effects is the same, although the *level* of effects varies slightly. The overall issue effects produce a net gain for the Republicans of 3.5 percentage points in contrast to the 7 point net advantage described earlier. More specifically, the Vietnam issue provided the largest net advantage to the Republicans (2 points), with most of that coming from the stable Republican voters over the 1968–72 time period. Of Nixon's total vote, 2.2 percent came from the loyalists on the Vietnam issue, with just over one percent coming from the switchers and new-transient voters. The crime and inflation issues also advantaged the incumbent, but the net effect was quite modest. Given the nature of the 1972 campaign, it seems highly unlikely that anything Senator McGovern could have done would have assured his victory.

Summary

No single issue dominated the electorate in 1972 as Vietnam had in 1968. At the same time, all of the issues worked in favor of Mr. Nixon. This was true, as well, for the issues crime and inflation, which could

TABLE 3.9 INFLUENCE OF PARTY PREFERRED ON ISSUES IN THE 1972 PRESIDENTIAL ELECTION*

		1972 Vote		
Voting Pattern	Nixon	Undecided[a] Nixon McGovern		McGovern
Vietnam				
Switch (N = 338)	0.6	14.4	6.0	0.2
Remain (N = 899)	2.2	37.5	18.6	0.9
Enter/Reenter (N = 311)	0.7	9.6	9.2	0.4
	3.5	61.5	33.8	1.5
Crime				
Switch (N = 338)	0.2	15.1	6.2	0.2
Remain (N = 899)	1.0	37.2	18.5	0.5
Enter/Reenter (N = 311)	0.3	9.5	9.7	---[b]
	1.5	61.8	34.4	0.7
Inflation				
Switch (N = 338)	0.2	14.9	6.3	---
Remain (N = 899)	0.9	37.7	19.0	0.3
Enter/Reenter (N = 311)	0.3	9.8	9.0	0.4
	1.4	62.4	34.3	0.7

(Total N = 1,548)

*Figures are as a percent of the total electorate. See text for further explanation.

[a]Undecided category includes those not citing a problem as "most important" or citing problems other than those under study.

[b]Less than .1 percent, or empty cell

plausibly be considered valence in nature, yet did not elicit the kinds of negative effects on support for the President that might have been expected. Consequently, these findings suggest some degree of prospective thinking by segments of the American electorate in 1972. Still, the unmediated issue effects were relatively small, although the mediated issue variables were consistently important. Nonetheless, no single issue could reasonably be said to have explained the election outcome. All the issues examined had a net positive impact on support for Nixon, although no policy mandate was evident. The election of 1972 seems to have been essentially a personal victory for the President and little more.

4

The 1976 Election:
The Emergence of Economic Issues

Whereas 1972 had witnessed a landslide victory for the Republican presidential candidate, the 1976 election was one of the closest, and perhaps most unusual, elections in U.S. history. Two candidates, virtually unknown outside their own states only four years earlier, contested for the presidency. As suggested in Chapter 1, the 1972 election victory had been seen by some as representing the long-awaited realignment of political forces, at least at the national level. Any talk of realignment, however, was rather quickly ended by the Watergate scandal and the resignation of President Nixon in August of 1974, together with the unpopular pardoning of Nixon by his successor, Gerald Ford.

Ford, whose presidency had begun on such a promising note following President Nixon's resignation in August of 1974, never really recovered from the Nixon pardon and recession. While he had recorded a 71 percent approval rating just weeks after taking office, this had fallen to under 50 percent in September following the pardon and continued to decline gradually, but steadily, over the last year.[1] Nor was Ford helped by the continuing pressure of OPEC on oil prices, together with the continued deterioration in the economy. Ford's presidential approval ratings are shown in Figure 4.1.[2] Unemployment and inflation data are shown in Figure 4.2.[3] By early 1976, it was clear that the presidential nomination contest in both parties was wide open. On the Republican side, Ronald Reagan was preparing what would prove to be a formidable challenge to President Ford, while within the Democratic party a number of relative unknowns vied for the nomination.

The Republican nomination battle, in particular, provided for high drama during the winter and spring. Ford began 1976 in serious trouble, which had probably helped entice Reagan into the race against an incumbent president. A January Gallup poll had given Ford a 39 percent approval rating, with 40 percent of those surveyed disapproving of his performance.[4]

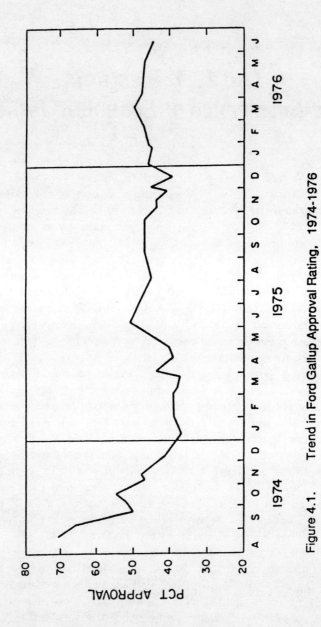

Figure 4.1.   Trend in Ford Gallup Approval Rating, 1974-1976

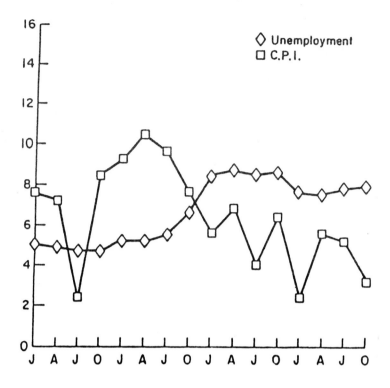

Figure 4.2.   Trends in Inflation and Unemployment, 1973-1976

It was also evident that, even if Ford could stave off the Reagan challenge, the Democrats would probably offer much stronger competition than they had in 1972. Voters in the winter of 1976 described the Democrats as better able to solve what they perceived to be the most important problem facing the nation by a 40 to 18 percent margin; moreover, the Democrats were perceived overwhelmingly—by margins of 23 and 47 percent—as being best able to deal with inflation and unemployment, respectively.[5] Gallup surveys consistently showed these two issues dominating the public consciousness. Unemployment had been gaining steadily in importance since 1974, when it was cited by only 3 percent of Gallup respondents, compared to 23 percent by January of that year.[6]

The Reagan campaign, which had suffered an early setback in New Hampshire, rallied in March and April and appeared at one point to be within striking distance of the nomination. Reagan's conservative positions on issues ranging from defense to social welfare appealed strongly to the conservative activists in the Republican party, while Ford's moderation was anathema to some. The campaign for the Republican nomination was the closest in decades, with Ford finally managing to eke out a victory. The battle, however, left the Republicans dispirited and divided, a condition which even the relatively uneventful convention could not fully repair.

On the Democratic side, Jimmy Carter, the former governor of Georgia, very quickly emerged as the front runner. Carter's campaign theme of restoring integrity to government was embodied in his call for "a government as good and as honest and as decent and as competent and as compassionate and as filled with love as are the American people."[7] In pushing this theme, other issues were somewhat muted, although surveys suggested that the twin economic concerns of inflation and unemployment remained at or near the top of the country's problem list. Indeed, throughout 1976 these two issues seemed to overwhelm other possible concerns facing the electorate.[8] Other surveys showed that among those issues most likely to influence the vote—inflation, unemployment and crime—the lack of foreign policy issues was striking. This led pollster George Gallup to suggest that, for the first time since 1936, a presidential election was not dominated by a single issue pertaining to peace, war, or foreign affairs.[9]

The American presence in Vietnam had ended in early 1973 with the signing in Paris of peace agreements by the warring parties. With the collapse of Vietnam in the spring of 1975 following a massive North Vietnamese offensive, Congress had refused President Ford's request for assistance. After the South Vietnamese and American defeat, Americans seemed anxious to forget the entire tragic episode of our involvement in Southeast Asia. Americans seemed to turn inward and turned a deaf ear to Ford's appeals for U.S. assistance to anti-Marxist rebels in Angola.

Carter, facing no unified opposition, went on to win the Democratic nomination with a series of primary victories in early June. Virtually all polls suggested a landslide for Carter. One Gallup survey taken in June just before the Democratic convention showed Carter defeating Ford 55 to 37 percent.[10] With the Democratic nomination fight in effect concluded by early June, and also perhaps because of the marked lack of any really significant issues dividing the party, the convention was characterized by a harmony which had been notably lacking in 1968 and 1972.

The general election campaign began with the Republican ticket of Ford and Dole the decided underdogs. For the first time since Herbert Hoover's defeat in 1932, it appeared likely that an incumbent president would be denied reelection (or in this case, election). Carter began the campaign with a huge lead in the polls. The Gallup poll showed Carter with a 33 percent lead after the Democratic convention, a lead which was impressive even given the fact that the Republicans had yet to formally select their ticket. At the end of August, just following the Republican convention, Carter still held what appeared to be an insurmountable 18 percent lead in the Gallup survey.[11] Carter, during this period, continued with the same themes developed in the nomination campaign. These basically portrayed Carter as the "anti-establishment" candidate who could restore faith and trust in government. Carter attempted to highlight this theme—i.e., by advocating governmental reorganization and reform.

President Ford adopted, at least initially, a "Rose Garden" strategy in which he was portrayed by his media advisors as the President who was too busy with the affairs of governing to campaign in the usual manner. Ford continued to narrow the gap in the polls, closing to within 6 points by the time of the second Ford-Carter debate. Ford's performance in the second debate, however, in which he had appeared to make the claim that Eastern Europe was not under Soviet domination, put the campaign on the defensive in a manner from which it never really recovered. By the time the Ford campaign had reoriented itself, it was too late. Even though the margin continued to close, with the last Gallup poll actually showing Ford in the lead for the first time by a 47 to 46 percentage, Carter managed to win by the narrow margin of 51 to 48 percent.[12]

Although issues were certainly discussed during the campaign, there is evidence that both candidates attempted to highlight their own qualities and personalities rather than stressing the possible issue differences between them. Carter, in fact, was often accused of fuzziness on a variety of issues, a tactic which may have been useful in avoiding any alienation of the major diverse elements of the Democratic coalition though he constantly hammered away at the ineptitude of the incumbent administration in its handling of the economy and other matters.[13]

While questions of personality and integrity seemed to dominate, there were still some important issues at work. As has already been shown, surveys consistently showed that economic problems were most important, particularly the problem of unemployment, which had risen dramatically during the 1974 recession and was still hovering at about 8 percent during the fall campaign. Unemployment has traditionally been the one issue most associated with the Democratic party. The coalition formed by Franklin Roosevelt had as its core of support the blue collar and union workers. When the party appeared to lose interest in "bread and butter" issues exemplified by unemployment, they had paid the price, as had seemingly happened to George McGovern in 1972. While the Democratic party as a whole was certainly more liberal than Carter on most issues, even Carter consistently advocated a more activist role for government in dealing with the problem of unemployment, including reluctant support for the Humphrey-Hawkins full employment measure which had recently been introduced in Congress.[14] Carter, however, tended to downplay specific policy proposals—with the exception of Humphrey-Hawkins—and generally tended to hammer away at the Republicans' poor stewardship of the economy. Inflation, on the other hand, had traditionally been an issue which Republicans had tended to stress. It may be that Ford's apparent reluctance to deal more forcefully with the unemployment issue, for fear of rekindling the inflationary pressures of the early 1970s, lost him crucial votes in the industrial Midwest and Northeast.

The majority party, as defined in terms of psychological attachment to a party, was victorious for the first time since 1964. As such, party identification appeared, at least superficially, to reassert itself in its impact on voter choice. Certainly the proportion of defectors from the Democratic party had declined dramatically. But, while the old Roosevelt coalition appeared, at least tentatively, to reassert itself in 1976, subsequent events would illustrate just how tenuous was Carter's victory coalition.

While Carter, just as Roosevelt, ran well in the South, he was heavily dependent upon black support. Indeed, in the South, Ford outpolled Carter among whites. The question of whether the 1976 election was an aberration will not be known for some time. Subsequent events do suggest that the nature of the Carter victory was tenuous at best and, in a broader sense, pointed out the fragile nature of the Democratic party coalition.

Rosenstone, citing the tentative nature of Southern allegiance to the Democratic party, has suggested that if racial or social welfare issues continue to possess the same degree of salience they had in previous elections (e.g., 1968 and, to a lesser extent, 1972), virtually any liberal Democratic nominee would lose the South and probably the election.[15] What may have been more important for Carter's ultimate fate, however, was the emergence of the twin issues of inflation and unemployment. Just as the old Roosevelt coalition was possible, owing to the severe unemployment of the early 1930s, so Carter's coalition, it could plausibly be argued, owed its existence in part to the recession of 1974–75. However, unlike the old New Deal coalition, the Carter coalition would come under severe strain by the late 1970s as economic problems continued to worsen.[16]

Individual Voting Behavior in 1976

In terms of the kinds of issues that were dealt with by the candidates, and which concerned the electorate, there was both continuity and change. Table 4.1 shows those problems identified by respondents to the 1976 Michigan cross-sectional study as being most important. Vietnam had obviously faded from public concern and was not cited by a *single* respondent as being the most important issue—thus illustrating the volatile nature of issue concerns in the electorate. Clearly, the trauma of Vietnam was at last beginning to recede. Indeed, "foreign affairs" in general were cited by just under one percent of the respondents.

What is most striking in Table 4.1 is the emergence of economic problems as the issues of major concern to the American electorate in 1976.[17] Among all those interviewed, more than 28 percent cited unemployment as most important, while inflation and general economic problems were mentioned by 24 and 8 percent, respectively. Crime was mentioned by nearly 7 percent. Hence, economic problems were cited by more than 60 percent of all respondents. The panel analysis for the 1976 data shows virtually the same results. Of those mentioning a problem in both 1972 and 1976, responses were within a percentage point or so of those obtained with the cross-sectional data (Table 4.2).

While the panel data will be used primarily to confirm the aggregate-level findings for the cross-sectional analyses, these individual-level data in Tables 4.1 and 4.2 clearly show that the kinds of problems identified as most important are not merely artifacts of the sampling procedures used in the study. That the same set of respondents could so dramatically alter their perceptions as to the most important issues facing the nation is solid evidence of the extreme volatility of issue concerns among the mass public. From the standpoint of this study, the size of the unemployment and inflation percentages is important because the high level of salience increases the potential for them being decisive in influencing outcomes of the election. This possibility is highlighted in Table 4.3. For those individuals capable of identifying a party best able to handle that problem, the Democrats were consistently favored. This difference is most pronounced for unemployment, where a healthy 52 percent favored the Democrats. However, 44 percent of those mentioning unemployment would not or could not decide which party was best able to handle this issue. Other issues showed party differentials on issues such as inflation, general economic problems and crime, with Democrats narrowly favored in each case.

These rather straightforward results strongly suggest that unemployment should have been a significant factor in explaining individual behavior *and* that it could contribute significantly to the outcome of the election because of its high salience and unidirectional nature. In contrast to the unemployment issue, inflation does not provide that kind of "tilt" toward one party. Indeed, while the Democrats were favored by a margin of 28 to 20 percent, a majority of 51 percent is undecided. While these

TABLE 4.1   MOST IMPORTANT ISSUES IN 1976 (CROSS SECTION)

Issue	N (unweighted)	Percentage Mentioning Problem as "Most Important"*	
		(1)	(2)
Unemployment	539	28.6	30.7
Inflation	467	24.7	26.8
Economy	153	8.1	8.7
Crime	131	6.9	7.5

N is the number of respondents.

*Column (1) includes all respondents whether or not they cited a problem as most important. Column (2) includes only those mentioning a problem.

TABLE 4.2   MOST IMPORTANT ISSUES IN 1976 (PANEL)

Issue	N	Percentage Mentioning Problem as "Most Important"*	
		(1)	(2)
Unemployment	332	26.4	28.5
Inflation	328	26.2	28.2
Economy	107	8.2	9.3
Crime	82	6.3	7.2

N is the number of respondents.

*Column (1) includes all respondents whether or not they cited a problem as most important. Column (2) includes only those mentioning a problem.

TABLE 4.3   PARTY PREFERRED IN 1976 ON MOST IMPORTANT ISSUES*

Issue	Republican N	%	Undecided N	%	Democrat N	%
Unemployment	24	(4.5)	236	(43.7)	279	(51.7)
Inflation	95	(20.3)	240	(51.3)	132	(28.2)
Economy	28	(18.3)	77	(50.3)	48	(31.3)
Crime	10	(7.6)	98	(74.8)	23	(17.5)

*N in each category is the number of respondents citing the party as best able to handle that particular issue. Numbers in parentheses are the percentages favoring that party on a particular issue.

preliminary findings suggest that concern for inflation is negatively related to individual support for Ford, a cautionary note is in order. We are uncertain of the direction of voting of those *undecided* as to party. But, if this were primarily a *Republican* issue, we should still see it working in favor of the Republicans. The other issues being examined, economy and crime, also exhibit a large percentage of undecided between parties. While the Democrats were favored by pluralities, the majority of those responding to these two issues were undecided and are likely to reduce the chance that they will have any major effect on election outcomes.

Overall, with the exception of unemployment, partisan linkages are not strong. Voters seem to have had difficulties differentiating the parties and their stands, which may well have been due to the ambiguity of the parties and candidates on the key issues. Further, a comparison of 1972 with 1976 illustrates the great fluidity of partisan linkages, suggesting the great potential for volatility of the American electoral process at the individual and aggregate levels.

The next step is to examine the bivariate relationship between the vote and issues, on the one hand, and vote and issue-party linkages, on the other. Both are crucial in informing us as to whether particular issues are important at the individual level. This, in turn, is critical for our aggregate-level analysis since it is a necessary, but not sufficient, condition for issues which significantly influence election outcomes also to be significant predictors of individual electoral choice.

Table 4.4 presents the initial findings for the relationship between individual electoral choice and issues. Here unemployment produces striking results. Among those mentioning unemployment as the most important problem, 69 percent voted for Carter, while among those *not* mentioning unemployment, Ford won by a margin of 57 to 43 percent, a 26 point difference. Other issues do not produce nearly so striking results. Taking the other two questions related to the economy, inflation and "general economic conditions," Ford was favored by a 55 to 45 percent margin among those who felt inflation was the most important problem, while Jimmy Carter held a 53 to 47 percent advantage among those not mentioning inflation—an overall eight point advantage for the Republican candidate on the inflation issue. A similar gap exists on the "general economic conditions" issue. Ford held a 57 to 43 percent advantage for those mentioning this as an issue, while Carter held a slender 51 to 49 percent advantage among those not mentioning it.

Lastly, the crime and disorder issue exhibited the smallest difference between the candidates in the "mentioned" and "not mentioned" category. Here, President Ford led Carter 55 to 45 percent among those mentioning crime-disorder as being most important, while Carter and Ford ran a virtual deadheat among those who fail to mention this as a major problem.

These findings suggest that unemployment is clearly the most influential predictor of *individual* voting choice, followed by inflation, general economic conditions, and crime-disorder. More important, the findings on unemployment—and, to a much lesser extent, inflation—suggest that these issues have a particularly good chance of strongly influencing the election *outcome*. Again, however, this was due not only to the relationship of issues to vote, but also to the high degree of salience found which unemployment and inflation held for people. Moreover, at least at the bivariate level, there is some evidence for an issue-priority effect concerning inflation.

As an alternative approach to examining issues, we look at the relationship between electoral choice and party preference on the selected issues (Table 4.5). As was the case in the previous chapter, they illustrate the overwhelming tendency of individuals who mention a party as best able to deal with a problem to *vote* for the candidate of that party. Whether one identifies the Republicans or Democrats as best able to handle a problem, that is the party voters are overwhelmingly likely to cite as having supported. When looking at unemployment, the most frequently mentioned issue, Ford was supported by 100 percent of those few (n=16) who believed the Republicans were best able to handle the unemployment question, while Carter was supported overwhelmingly (92 vs. 8 percent) by the large number (n=215) who believed the Democrats were best able to handle the problem. Virtually identical results obtain for inflation. For instance, among those favoring the Republican and Democratic positions on inflation, Ford and Carter were

TABLE 4.4 REPORTED PERCENTAGE VOTE FOR CANDIDATES IN 1976 BY SELECTED
MOST IMPORTANT ISSUES

Candidate	Unemployment NM	M	Inflation NM	M	Economy NM	M	Crime NM	M
Carter	43.4	68.5	52.7	44.6	51.2	43.0	50.9	44.8
Ford	56.6	31.5	47.3	55.4	48.8	57.0	49.1	55.2
(Total N=1,305)	934.0	371.0	955.0	350.0	1,191.0	114.0	1,218.0	87.0

- NM refers to those respondents <u>not mentioning</u> a problem as most
important.

- M refers to those respondents <u>mentioning</u> a particular issue as most
important.

NOTE: Percentages have been rounded to the nearest one-tenth percent.

TABLE 4.5 PARTY PREFERRED ON MOST IMPORTANT ISSUES IN 1976
AND PERCENTAGE VOTE FOR CANDIDATES

Issue	Party Preferred Republican %	Undecided* %	Democrat %
Unemployment			
Carter	--**	43.4	91.6
Ford	100.0	56.6	8.4
N	16.0	1,074.0	215.0
Inflation			
Carter	3.4	50.7	92.0
Ford	96.6	49.3	8.0
N	88.0	1,117.0	100.0
Economy			
Carter	--**	50.6	86.1
Ford	100.0	49.4	13.9
N	24.0	1,245.0	36.0
Crime			
Carter	--**	50.6	93.3
Ford	100.0	49.4	6.7
N	10.0	1,247.0	15.0

(Total N = 1,305)

*The "undecided" category includes those who did not mention
a problem, since we assume that those undecided between the
Republican and Democratic parties on an issue behave no
differently than those not citing a problem.

** refers to no cases in cells

favored by 97 to 3 and 92 to 8 percent, respectively. Similar findings obtain for the economy and crime-disorder issues, indicating that the issue-party variables are highly significant predictors of individual electoral choice. But, to stress a point made earlier, the impact on the election outcome will depend upon the salience of an issue *plus* its unidirectional character. Unemployment and possibly inflation, both typically viewed as valence issues, are the only issues which would appear to meet these criteria.

As with the 1972 election, electoral behavior in the 1976 election is examined using probit analysis. The results tend, for the most part, to confirm the more simple bivariate analyses. When one examines the influence of unmediated issues controlling for partisanship (Table 4.6), we find that unemployment is the one issue which produces a significant influence on voting behavior. Indeed, unemployment is the *only* issue which, by itself, produces any real impact on actual voting behavior. That is, those who cited unemployment as the most important problem facing the nation are significantly more unlikely to support the Republican party than those who do not mention unemployment.

Inflation approaches statistical significance and has a negative sign, indicating that concern over inflation is *negatively* related to a Republican vote, controlling for other variables. Recall that the earlier analysis for 1972 was suggestive of an issue-priority effect. The multivariate case suggests a reward-punishment model of voting. The other issues, "economy" and crime, had virtually no influence on voting behavior once partisanship is controlled. Overall, though, the additional variance explained by all issues together—beyond that explained by partisanship—is a paltry two percentage points. Although crime did not produce a statistically significant effect, it did work to Carter's benefit, even controlling for partisanship.

Most important is the finding that inflation (at the individual level) had a negative effect, a reversal of 1972. The Republicans do not appear to have "owned" this issue in 1976, possibly owing to the voters' remembrance of the inflationary surge in 1973–1974. A valence issue that worked to the incumbents' advantage four years earlier worked against them four years later.

As with 1972, the mediated issue-party variables produced quite strong results. The economy, inflation, and unemployment all generated very strong effects. Unemployment, although significant, provided a nearly identical effect when connected to party than without the party link. It should be noted that all signs are positive, simply indicating that those who believed the Republicans were best able to deal with an issue, such as inflation or unemployment, were significantly more

TABLE 4.6   PROBIT ESTIMATES OF EFFECTS OF PARTISANSHIP AND
ISSUE-PRIORITY VARIABLES ON 1976 VOTE

Variables	Model One	Model Two
Constant	0.322/(0.087)*	0.334/(0.066)*
Republican Party ID	0.969/(0.104)*	0.832/(0.114)*
Democratic Party ID	-0.982/(0.091)*	-0.892/(0.100)*
Unemployment	-0.525/(0.106)*	1.356/(0.144)*
Inflation	-0.166/(0.104)	1.555/(0.166)*
Economy	-0.101/(0.153)	1.265/(0.268)*
Crime	-0.118/(0.171)	- - -
N = 1272		
Estimated R^2	.42	.62
R^2 increment**	.02	.22
Rho	.52	.62
% Correctly classified	.76	.81

*P $\leq$ .05

**R^2 increment refers to additional variance explained by the
issue variables over and beyond that explained by partisanship alone.

likely to vote Republican than those who did not.[18] These findings again
illustrate the potency of prospective orientations on voting behavior.

Individual Voting
and the 1976 Election Outcome

As with the 1972 analysis, the next step is to examine the aggregate-
level dynamics of the 1976 election. Table 4.7 provides a general
breakdown of the eligible 1976 electorate with regard to the sources of
change between 1968 and 1972. More than 47 percent reported voting
for the same party between 1972 and 1976, a 5 percent gain over 1972.
The total number of switchers, 13 percent, was nearly the same. As will
be seen, though, this group plays a major role in determining the outcome

of the 1976 election. "Floating" voters who moved in and out of the electorate—the transients—constituted a slightly higher percentage of the electorate—8.6 percent—than in 1972. Finally, the new voters constituted nearly 4 percent of the actual electorate. Among the nonvoters, 27.2 percent acknowledged not voting in this particular election. Of this group, most—17 percent of the potential electorate—were consistent nonvoters, while about 11 percent claimed to have voted in the 1972 race but "dropped out" in 1976, or were newly eligible but failed to vote.

When the turnover table (Table 4.8) is examined, one finds dramatically different results from those observed in 1972. The Republican candidate, Mr. Ford, held only 66 percent of the vote that had gone to President Nixon four years earlier. This represents a 14 percent decline from the 1968–72 performance of Mr. Nixon in *maintaining* Republican voters over the two elections. At the same time, while Nixon in 1972 suffered the loss of only 10 percent shifting to McGovern, the percentage of those who supported the Democratic ticket in both 1972 and 1976—78 percent of the electorate—compares quite favorably with the 80 percent Nixon attained in 1972 for the 1968–72 elections.

Among the 1972 nonvoters, a full 66 percent did not vote in 1976. But, among those who *did* vote, Carter held a more than 2 to 1 advantage. Clearly, the 1976 election did not activate the less committed elements of the potential electorate. Indeed, there are few differences between 1972 and 1976. The pattern of voting by newly eligible voters held few surprises. Fifty-three percent reported failing to participate, which one would expect given the previous pattern of political participation and non-participation among the young.

Issues and the 1976 Election Outcome

The impact of issues on the 1976 election outcome is displayed in Table 4.9. As could be surmised from the closeness of the election, as well as the examination of the turnover table, no single candidate dominated, although certain issues clearly worked in a unidirectional fashion to the benefit of one party or another. Governor Carter received most of the switchers' votes, just as Nixon had done four years earlier. Carter received 87 and 77 percent of the vote, respectively, of those voters who most frequently mentioned issues of unemployment and inflation. He also gained nearly three-quarters of the switchers on the issue of "general economic problems." Not surprisingly, the one issue which worked to Mr. Ford's advantage among the switchers was crime-disorder, with 73 percent citing this problem supporting the President. Unfortunately for Mr. Ford, this problem was not salient with a sufficient

TABLE 4.7   SOURCES OF PERCENT CHANGE IN THE 1972-1976
ELECTIONS (1972-1976 CROSS SECTION)

Category	Electorate
Remain[1]	47.4%
Switchers[2]	13.0%
Transients[3]	8.6%
New Voters[4]	3.3%
Transient and Newly Eligible Nonvoters[5]	11.1%
Nonvoters[6]	16.6%
(Total N = 1,744)	100.0%

[1]Those voting for same party in both 1972 and 1976.

[2]Those who switch from one party candidate to another between 1972 and 1976.

[3]Those voting in 1976 who were eligible to vote in 1972 but abstained.

[4]Those voting in 1976 who were ineligible to vote in 1972.

[5]Those eligible to vote in 1976 who voted in 1972 but abstained, and those newly eligible who failed to vote.

[6]Those who failed to vote in both 1972 and 1976.

TABLE 4.8   TURNOVER TABLE, 1972-1976 (1976 VOTING PATTERNS BY 1972 VOTING PATTERNS) CROSS SECTION

1976 Vote	1972 Vote			
	Nixon	McGovern	Non Voter	Ineligible
Ford	66.1	11.2	10.5	21.6
Carter	23.1	77.9	23.7	25.6
Abstained	10.8	10.9	65.8	52.8
(Total N = 1,744)	778.0	402.0	439.0	125.0

chi-square = 981.49m d.f. = 6, p < .001

Cramer's V = .53

TABLE 4.9   EFFECT OF ISSUES IN THE 1976 PRESIDENTIAL
ELECTION*

Voting Pattern	1976 Vote	
	Ford	Carter
Unemployment		
Switch (N = 225)	13 (0.7)	87 (4.6)
Remain (N = 827)	41 (7.2)	59 (10.3)
Enter/Reenter (N = 209)	14 (0.7)	86 (4.2)
	8.6	19.1
Inflation		
Switch (N = 225)	23 (1.1)	77 (4.2)
Remain (N = 827)	70 (11.0)	30 (4.8)
Enter/Reenter (N = 209)	44 (1.5)	56 (2.0)
	13.6	11.0
Economy		
Switch (N = 225)	29 (0.5)	71 (1.0)
Remain (N = 827)	65 (4.0)	35 (2.2)
Enter/Reenter (N = 209)	50 (1.0)	50 (1.0)
	5.5	4.2
Crime		
Switch (N = 225)	73 (0.6)	27 (0.2)
Remain (N = 827)	67 (3.0)	33 (1.5)
Enter/Reenter (N = 209)	46 (0.5)	54 (0.5)
	4.1	2.2

(Total N = 1,261)

*Figures not in parentheses represent percentage support for
candidate; figures in parentheses are vote as percentage of
entire electorate.

number of voters to influence the outcome to any significant extent.
Carter also received the support of the bulk of new and transient voters,
with his most dramatic showing coming from the unemployment issue;
86 percent of all new and transient voters reported voting for Carter.

A markedly different trend is evident when the loyalists are examined.
Ford carried this group by very healthy margins on every single issue,
with the sole—and for him, unfortunate—exception of unemployment.
While the President was carrying the loyalists on the inflation, general
economic problem, and crime issues by margins ranging from 65 to 70
percent, Carter was carrying this group on the unemployment issue by
a margin of 59 to 41 percent. Clearly, unemployment had an enormous
effect on the election, producing a net overall gain for Carter of nearly
11 percent.

In contrast, Mr. Ford had net gains on each of the other issues. Inflation produced a net gain for Ford of about 2.6 percent with virtually all deriving from loyalists who had voted Republican in 1972. Among switchers and new and transient voters, inflation worked marginally against Mr. Ford. It will be recalled that the individual-level analysis showed inflation negatively related to support for Mr. Ford. The reversal at the aggregate level illustrates the danger of blindly inferring similar relationships at the two levels of analysis. Since multicollinearity was not especially high, which would make unreliable the estimates, the findings may be due to the fact that those concerned with inflation were likely to vote Republican anyway. As for the crime-disorder issue, he had small net advantages among both switchers and loyalists. On the "economy" variable, Ford gained a net overall advantage over Carter of 1.3 percent of the vote, with all of the gain coming from loyalists. However, as the table shows, Mr. Ford was actually hurt by the switchers, who gave Carter a marginal advantage. Overall, then, unemployment worked to the benefit of Jimmy Carter, providing him with an overall net advantage of nearly 7 percent among all issues. Unemployment, in short, appears to have been a decisive factor in explaining the 1976 election outcome. But since the individual-level findings were suggestive of a reward-punishment effect, it appears that the electorate was responding to the perceived inadequate performance of the incumbent Republican administration in addressing this issue. There is little evidence that the electorate was responding to clear policy proposals from Governor Carter.

As was the case with the 1972 data, the influence of the issue-party mediated effects should be examined. It will be recalled that in 1972 this particular analysis indicated that issue effects were slightly less important than they initially appeared. This is not the case in 1976. The four most frequent issues combined (see Table 4.10) generate a pro-Democratic net advantage of about 11 points, with the economic issues of unemployment, inflation, and "general economic problems" showing a net advantage of about 12 points. However, the one issue with a clear and unambiguous pro-Democratic effect was unemployment, which produced a net effect of approximately 12 points in favor of Jimmy Carter.

What is especially striking about the dynamics of the unemployment issue is the marked influence of the switchers from 1972 to 1976 as well as the influence of those just entering or—in the case of "transient" voters—reentering the electorate. Switchers and the new-transient voters produced a net pro-Democratic vote gain of nearly 3.4 and 2.7 percent, respectively. Unemployment was almost certainly the single most salient issue among these groups. Indeed, the net effects generated by these

TABLE 4.10 INFLUENCE OF PARTY PREFERRED ON ISSUES IN THE
1976 PRESIDENTIAL ELECTION*

Voting Pattern	Ford	Undecided[a] Ford	Carter	Carter
Unemployment				
Switch (N = 225)	0.1	3.2	10.7	3.5
Remain (N = 827)	1.0	38.8	16.2	8.1
Enter/Reenter (N = 209)	0.2	5.4	7.2	2.9
	1.3	47.4	34.1	14.5
Inflation				
Switch (N = 225)	0.3	3.3	12.0	1.8
Remain (N = 827)	5.8	34.4	21.5	3.1
Enter/Reenter (N = 209)	0.5	3.3	12.0	1.1
	6.6	41.0	45.5	6.0
Economy				
Switch (N = 225)	0.7	3.8	13.5	--[b]
Remain (N = 827)	1.5	39.0	23.4	1.3
Enter/Reenter (N = 209)	0.1	5.3	10.4	0.3
	2.3	48.1	47.3	1.6
Crime				
Switch (N = 225)	---	3.5	14.1	0.1
Remain (N = 827)	0.6	40.0	24.2	0.5
Enter/Reenter (N = 209)	0.7	5.7	10.4	0.3
	0.7	49.2	48.7	0.9

(Total N = 1,261)

*Figures are as a percent of the total electorate. See text for further explanation.

[a]Undecided category includes those not citing a problem as "most important" or citing problems other than those under study.

[b]Less than .1 percent, or empty cell.

groups were in fact marginally more than was the case for the "stable" voters who supported the same party between 1972 and 1976.

Also, the inflation issue again had a net positive effect on the Republican ticket. However, in this case net advantage was a little less than 1.0 percent. The distribution of opinion on the inflation issue illustrated how relative importance at the individual-level does not help to explain election outcomes. Among those undecided on this issue, Carter had an advantage of 45.5 to 41 percent for a net gain of 4.5 points. The other issues of "general economic problems" and "crime" had, as with the previous analyses, extremely modest effects. The aggregate analyses to this point indicate that the one truly decisive issue in the 1976 election was unemployment.

1972–1976 Panel Analysis

To confirm our cross-sectional findings for 1976, an example of the 1972–76 panel is in order. The chief advantage for the purposes of this study is that one does not have to rely upon the *reported* previous vote. Instead, one can use the vote preference (if any) reported at the time of the actual study. The makeup of both the potential and actual electorate was found to be quite close to that obtained for our cross-sectional study. More striking than the composition of the electorate, which was quite similar to the cross-section, the turnover table (these tables not shown) revealed almost identical patterns of voting to those shown earlier. This makes us confident that our interpretation of the 1976 election, and more generally of other elections for which panel data were not available, are valid. The findings also parallel earlier results demonstrating the aggregate issue effects on the election. One would not expect the issue effects to be totally identical, and they are not. More important, though, are the general directional effects. The unemployment and inflation issues produced an aggregate pro-Democratic effect very similar to the earlier analyses (Tables 4.11 and 4.12). Other problems studied were virtually identical to the cross-section, with "general economic problems" and "crime" demonstrating minimal variation with the cross-section.

Carter did consistently better among switchers on all issues, although, owing to the salience of unemployment and inflation, these issues produce the largest effects. New voters and transients produced only very marginal effects, although in each case Carter also benefitted. The most pronounced aggregate effect for this group is also seen on the unemployment issue, where Carter achieved a net gain of 1.7 percent of the vote among this element of the electorate. In terms of *overall* effects, the unemployment issue worked overwhelmingly in favor of the Democratic nominee, generating a net advantage to Mr. Carter of about 7.5 percent. At the same time, inflation effects are essentially cancelled out. As was noted in the cross-sectional study, which once again produces results quite similar to these, this differs from the findings in which we merely looked at the relation between most important issue and election outcomes. There, it was shown that, while unemployment had a strong unidirectional effect in favor of the Democrats, inflation had a moderate unidirectional effect in favor of the Republicans. Those citing inflation as an issue, but

TABLE 4.11 EFFECT OF ISSUES IN THE 1976 PRESIDENTIAL
ELECTION* (PANEL)

| | 1976 Vote | |
Voting Pattern	Ford	Carter
Unemployment		
Switch (N = 204)	14 (1.5)	86 (6.4)
Remain (N = 572)	39 (4.3)	61 (6.2)
Enter/Reenter (N = 109)	30 (1.3)	70 (3.0)
	7.1	15.6
Inflation		
Switch (N = 204)	24 (2.6)	76 (4.8)
Remain (N = 572)	61 (11.4)	39 (7.4)
Enter/Reenter (N = 109)	50 (1.6)	50 (1.6)
	15.6	13.8
Economy		
Switch (N = 204)	14 (0.3)	86 (2.0)
Remain (N = 572)	67 (4.8)	33 (2.4)
Enter/Reenter (N = 109)	0 (---)a	100 (0.1)
	5.1	4.5
Crime		
Switch (N = 204)	83 (1.1)	17 (0.2)
Remain (N = 572)	70 (2.8)	30 (1.2)
Enter/Reenter (N = 109)	60 (0.6)	40 (0.4)
	4.5	1.8

(Total N = 885)

*Figures not in parentheses represent percentage support for candidate; figures in parentheses are vote as percentage of entire electorate.

aLess than .1 percent, or empty cell

undecided as to party most competent to deal with it, supported the status quo by supporting Mr. Ford.

Summary

Of primary interest—as with the other cases—is determining which, if any, issues actually affected the *outcome* of the election. The analysis clearly demonstrates that, although unemployment and general economic problems were important at the individual level in explaining voting behavior, the one issue which affected the outcome of the 1976 election was unemployment. *Only* unemployment operated dramatically in favor of one party, the Democrats. Perhaps, not surprisingly, the *one* issue

TABLE 4.12 INFLUENCE OF PARTY PREFERRED ON ISSUES IN THE
1976 PRESIDENTIAL ELECTION* (PANEL)

Voting Pattern	Ford	Undecided[a] Ford	Carter	Carter
Unemployment				
Switch (N = 204)	---[b]	4.2	13.3	4.7
Remain (N = (572)	0.7	38.5	16.0	7.2
Enter/Reenter (N = 109)	0.1	4.7	4.5	2.5
	0.8	47.4	33.8	14.4
Inflation				
Switch (N = 204)	0.2	4.3	15.1	3.0
Remain (N = (572)	6.6	35.5	20.2	3.1
Enter/Reenter (N = 109)	0.4	4.6	6.0	1.1
	7.2	44.4	41.3	7.2
Economy				
Switch (N = 204)	0.1	4.3	16.6	1.4
Remain (N = (572)	2.0	38.5	21.7	1.6
Enter/Reenter (N = 109)	---	5.1	6.8	0.2
	2.1	47.9	45.1	3.2
Crime				
Switch (N = 204)	---	4.4	17.7	0.2
Remain (N = (572)	0.5	40.2	22.7	0.6
Enter/Reenter (N = 109)	---	5.1	6.8	0.2
	0.5	49.7	47.2	1.0

(Total N = 885)

*Figures are as a percent of the total electorate. See text
for further explanation.

[a]Undecided category includes those not citing a problem as
"most important" or citing problems other than those under
study.

[b]Less than .1 percent, or empty cell

which was significant—highly so—at the individual level was the issue
which best explained the election outcome.

While inflation would seemingly take on the qualities of a valence
issue, this issue produced only minimum effects at the aggregate level
in benefitting Mr. Ford. James Alt has suggested that the presence of a
valence issue does not necessarily mean the issue will affect an election's
outcome, since those potentially vulnerable can point out various shortcomings and inconsistencies in their opponent's position.[19] Occasionally,
such strategies, if adopted, may be for nought because they are only

effective within a relatively constrained range. Thus, valence issues may work dramatically against the incumbents and be decisive in determining the election outcome. President Ford in 1976 was clearly unable to finesse the question of unemployment. In the final analysis, he was forced to stand on his administration's handling of that issue. This may also be true even if we assume voters capable of distinguishing the issue priorities of the parties. Even if voters historically have believed Republicans better able to handle inflation, let us say, the poor inflation performance of 1973–74 may have served to weaken their credibility on this issue.

Can one say that the election represented a policy mandate? The findings suggest not. The 1976 election seems to have been a referendum on the prior performance of the incumbent, as typified by the valence-type issues of inflation and especially unemployment. There was no "message" in 1976 other than the voters were unhappy with the economy and expected something to be done about it.

5

The 1980 Election: The Economy Revisited

Political scientists are still attempting to determine, eight years after the fact, the significance of the 1980 election. Was this election the signal for a massive realignment of electoral forces and the final demise of the New Deal coalition, or was it an aberration, the result of a number of short-term forces, both issues and candidate related? The Carter administration, which took office in January of 1977, faced a seemingly endless succession of crises. Carter appeared plagued by continued difficulties with Congress. The belief increased that the President was inept—a belief held by the public and Congress. This problem plagued Carter through his entire administration.

There were a variety of reasons for Carter's problems with Congress. The dispersal of power and authority, resulting from the growth of the committee and subcommittee system, together with the decline of party discipline, were all factors beyond Carter's control.[1] Other instances, however, such as the proposed Carter "hit list" of waterway projects, represented seemingly inept assaults on policy areas in which Congress had traditionally dominated. Other problems faced by Carter included the Burt Lance resignation in September of 1977 and the increased Soviet assertiveness in the Third World.

All of these problems, though, were minor compared to those of the economy which began to deteriorate in 1978 and 1979. Massive oil price increases were being blamed for increased inflation, while simultaneously discouraging an expansion in employment. The problem of stagflation, which had just appeared on the scene in the early 1970s, strongly reasserted itself. The "misery index," the sum of both the unemployment and inflation rates, had reached 18 points by early 1980.[2] This in itself began to raise suspicions very early in the election season that Carter could be highly vulnerable to a Republican challenge.[3] Figure 5.1 shows the general downward trends from 1977–80 in President Carter's approval rating.[4] Figure 5.2 provides data on unemployment and inflation during this same period.[5] Just as Carter had appeared to use the state of the

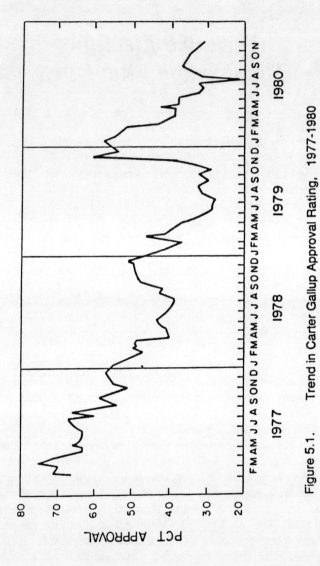

Figure 5.1.   Trend in Carter Gallup Approval Rating, 1977-1980

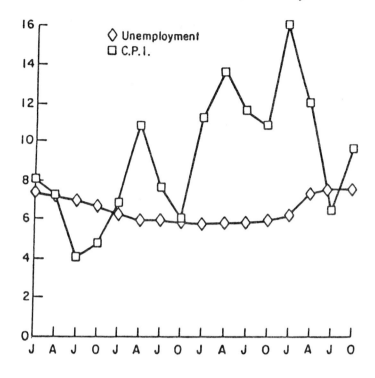

Figure 5.2.   Trends in Inflation and Unemployment,
1977-1980

economy as an effective weapon against Gerald Ford, the potential
existed for the same problem to occur with the Democratic incumbent.

In addition to economic problems, foreign policy difficulties continued
to trouble the President. Soviet intervention in the Horn of Africa,
involving support for the new Marxist Ethiopian regime, suggested an
increasingly assertive and confident Soviet leadership. This was soon
followed in September of 1979 by revelations of a Soviet brigade in
Cuba, and then finally by the takeover of the American Embassy in
Teheran on November 4, 1979. The Russian invasion of Afghanistan
occurred in December of that same year. All of this, of course, was in
addition to the steady pressure being exerted by OPEC—a pressure felt
in the inflation and unemployment rates—and typified by rising gasoline
prices. These events all served to reinforce the uneasy feeling that
Americans were becoming increasingly vulnerable in a hostile world.[6]
The combined impact of events, both foreign and domestic, contributed
to a feeling that things were out of control. This was also reflected in

surveys which showed an increase of public dissatisfaction with the performance of both governmental and non-governmental institutions.[7]

By late 1979, it was almost inevitable that Carter would have a difficult time with his reelection. Not only would he have to defend his record against the Republican challenger, he would also have to fight to win his own party's nomination. By the fall of 1979 many prominent Democrats, both elected and non-elected, were beginning to place pressure on Senator Edward Kennedy to challenge Carter for the nomination. Surveys as late as October of 1979 showed Kennedy leading Carter among Democrats in every region by substantial margins and Carter showing huge "negative" ratings.[8]

Kennedy's entrance into the race was followed by an immediate decline in his fortunes. Most important was the seizure of the American Embassy in Teheran on November 4, precisely one year from the date of the next presidential election. Within a month of the seizure, Carter had made a seemingly miraculous recovery. One survey showed 76 percent approval for the President's handling of the Iranian hostage crisis, and this surge of approval was reflected in significant leads which Carter held over both Edward Kennedy and Ronald Reagan. The Iranian hostage crisis was soon followed by the Soviet invasion of Afghanistan. This provided Carter with the backdrop against which he could display his leadership abilities which many had perceived to be significantly lacking.[9]

Unfortunately for Carter, this surge in approval proved to be rather ephemeral. By late January, the hostage crisis continued unresolved. The Soviets continued with their occupation of Afghanistan. Other politicians became bolder in their criticisms of Carter's handling of the crises, and his approval began to suffer (see Figure 5.1). Support for his handling of the Iranian crisis, in particular, began to decline and served to illustrate how rapidly public opinion could change.[10]

But although Carter's overall support was to decline throughout the spring and summer, the initial surge attained early in the year proved sufficient to carry him to the nomination, even though he was unable to drive Senator Edward Kennedy from the race. In more general terms, the candidates differed substantially in their assessment of how much government could be expected to do.[11] This notion of the need for government restraint was, of course, to be a major criticism Reagan would make against the Democrats in the general election campaign.

As the campaign moved into the general election phase, Carter was in an extremely vulnerable position. His opponent, Ronald Reagan, had swept through the primaries with relative ease. After being surprised in the Iowa caucuses, he achieved a string of victories which effectively eliminated his major rival, George Bush, from contention. The harmonious

Republican convention in July had added to the perception that the Republican ticket would be a formidable one.

The issues seemed to be working against the Democrats. By September of 1980, inflation, unemployment, and international problems were cited by voters as most important. Of those, 61 percent cited inflation. More important for Democrats, Republicans consistently rated as the party best able to deal with these problems. For instance, Republicans scored 44–29 percent over Democrats on the issue of inflation, 41–32 on the issue of unemployment, and 55–28 on the general issue of defense. Only on the question of compassion and keeping the U.S. out of war did the Democrats rate higher among the public. Overall, the most salient issues were working to the advantage of the Republicans.[12]

The Democrats, however, may have come increasingly to be perceived as the party of special interests. The reforms of the early 1970s had certainly led to increased opportunities for political participation by various groups. But the negative side indicated an increased perception that these particular groups—blacks, feminists, gays, etc.—were dictating party policy.

Reagan, although certainly seeking the support of the social conservatives such as Jerry Falwell's Moral Majority, nonetheless did not seek too close a relationship with these groups. Reagan's strategy was to keep the chief focus on the economy and the economic malaise the country was experiencing, while at the same time remaining somewhat vague about his own policies. Carter, attempting to avoid having the election become a referendum on the economy, attacked Reagan's alleged lack of compassion for the poor, elderly, and racial minorities, and hinted that Reagan's conservative policies would produce racial, religious, and regional fragmentation if he was elected to the presidency. Carter also emphasized the "peace" issue, suggesting in his speeches that Reagan simply did not understand the complexities of world politics, and that his simplistic anti-communist slogans were not sufficient guides to foreign policy. Reagan, on the other hand, continued to emphasize inflation and unemployment rates, together with what he claimed was a dangerous decline in U.S. military strength.[13]

The question of Iran was treated gingerly by both candidates. Carter wanted to avoid being seen as using the hostages' predicament for his own political gain. Reagan, for similar reasons, avoided the issue. In addition he wished to avoid leaving himself open to the charge that he was meddling in a dangerous area of foreign policy best left untouched by any challenger.

Of all events prior to the election, perhaps the one most crucial was the second debate in Cleveland on October 28. The first debate in September between Reagan and Anderson had been inconclusive and suffered from the non-attendance of Carter, who feared enhancing Anderson's credibility and vote drawing power at the expense of himself and the Democrats. The second debate, however, held all the elements for high drama. With surveys showing the election outcome too close to call, the debate was seen as an opportunity by both men to solidify their already existing support and to attract undecided voters. Though Carter showed a clear knowledge of the issues, Reagan emerged the clear winner in political terms, though not necessarily through winning debating points. Reagan managed to portray himself as a genial and friendly individual who could not possibly be the militant extremist the Democrats had portrayed. He finessed the questions about his proposed social welfare policies by suggesting that his quotes had been taken out of context. And perhaps most damaging for Carter were his frequent condemnations of the state of the economy. Carter was ultimately bested when Reagan concluded with the rhetorical question: "Are you better off today than you were four years ago?" a question which Carter had found useful in 1976.

Even though public surveys continued to indicate a very close race, the outcome was stunning. Reagan's popular and electoral vote landslide represented, at a minimum, a sweeping repudiation of the incumbent and his stewardship of the last four years. Whether it represented a sweeping mandate for a conservative policy agenda is more problematic. At a minimum, it seems voters were saying that the incumbent's handling of the key issues during the previous four years had been inadequate and that a change was necessary.

Individual Voting Behavior in 1980

As with the comparison of 1976 with the 1972 data, a comparison of 1980 with the former produces some startling changes in the kind of problems of primary concern to the American people. As shown in Table 5.1, inflation and unemployment were identified as the two most important economic problems, with worries about Iran and military preparedness also occupying a prominent position among the concerns of voters. However, while in 1976 unemployment had been identified as the single most important issue, by 1980 inflation had emerged as the dominant concern among voters. By 1980, a full 41 percent of those mentioning a problem referred to economic issues, with inflation being the single most salient. Inflation was cited by 32 percent of all those mentioning a problem. Iran, unemployment, and defense were far behind. Iran was mentioned by 14 percent; unemployment by only 10 percent. Among the issues mentioned, inflation and unemployment would be identified as valence-type issues. Iran, which was almost certainly picking up voter concern and disgust with the hostage crisis, is somewhat more problematic and should probably be treated also as a valence issue. It seems plausible to assume that voters simply wanted a resolution to the crisis—a focus on "ends"—and were not particularly concerned with how this was to be done. Only defense, which expressed concern for perceived U.S. military vulnerability, should be treated clearly as a positional issue.

As for those able to identify the party favored on those issues cited as "most important," Table 5.2 reveals some interesting features. In each instance, the Republicans were favored by a plurality, though in one case the Republican party did attain majority support. The inflation issue, which had emerged as the single most frequently cited problem, worked overwhelmingly to the Republicans' advantage. Forty-nine percent of those mentioning inflation favored the Republican party. A miniscule 6 percent favored the Democrats and 45 percent were undecided. The salience of the inflation issue, combined with the overwhelming Republican advantage, suggests that it had great potential, not only for being highly significant at the individual-level of analysis, but also in explaining the election outcome.

Unemployment provides a stark example of the highly variable nature of issue-party links. Whereas in 1976 the Democrats had been favored by a huge margin, by 1980 the Republicans were favored by 28–17 percent. The majority of those citing unemployment were undecided between Republicans and Democrats. This in itself suggests that, while unemployment may still be significant at the individual level, its declining salience from 1976, together with the party link alterations, radically reduced its ability to generate major changes in the election outcome.

The other issues, Iran and defense, provided a Republican advantage. Thirty percent of those mentioning Iran believed the Republicans more competent to deal with the issue, in comparison to 11 percent favoring the Democrats. Nonetheless, 59 percent were undecided. In contrast, defense is an excellent example of an issue which appeared to work substantially to the benefit of the Republicans and, in fact, should be a good predictor of individual behavior. However, it should have limited aggregate effects due to its relatively low salience. Still, Iran and defense issues together illustrate the damage done to Carter and to the Democrats in 1980 by perceived weakness displayed by Carter in his handling of international affairs and foreign policy.

The findings shown in Table 5.3 indicate that approximately 64 percent of all those citing inflation as the most important problem supported Reagan and the Republican party. This is a shift of 9 percent in a pro-Republican direction since 1976. Even more interesting is that nearly 53

TABLE 5.1   MOST IMPORTANT ISSUES IN 1980

Issue	N	Percentage Mentioning Problem as "Most Important"*	
		(1)	(2)
Inflation	446	31.6	32.9
Iran	201	14.2	14.8
Unemployment	138	9.8	10.1
Defense	82	5.8	6.0

N is the number of respondents.

*Column (1) includes all respondents whether or not they
cited a problem as most important. Column two includes only
those mentioning a problem.

TABLE 5.2   PARTY PREFERRED IN 1980 ON MOST IMPORTANT ISSUES*

Issue	Republican N %	Undecided N %	Democrat N %
Inflation	220 (49.3)	200 (44.8)	26 (5.8)
Iran	61 (30.3)	118 (58.7)	22 (10.9)
Unemployment	38 (27.5)	77 (55.8)	23 (16.7)
Defense	49 (59.7)	29 (35.4)	4 (4.9)

*N in each category is the number of respondents citing the
party as best able to handle that particular issue. Numbers
in parentheses are the percentages favoring that party on a
particular issue.

TABLE 5.3 REPORTED PERCENTAGE VOTE FOR CANDIDATES IN 1980 BY SELECTED
MOST IMPORTANT ISSUES

	Inflation		Iran		Unemployment		Defense	
	NM	M	NM	M	NM	M	NM	M
Carter	47.2	36.2	42.9	47.1	41.5	63.3	44.0	35.7
Reagan	52.8	63.8	57.1	52.9	58.5	36.7	56.0	64.3
(Total N=871)	578.0	293.0	750.0	121.0	792.0	79.0	815.0	56.0

- NM refers to those respondents <u>not mentioning</u> a problem as most
important.

- M refers to those respondents <u>mentioning</u> a particular issue as most
important.

NOTE: Percentages have been rounded to the nearest one-tenth percent.

percent of those who did not cite inflation as a problem reported voting
for Reagan, a 10-point Republican advantage on the inflation issue.

In contrast to inflation, the findings for unemployment demonstrate
the continued salience of the Depression, at least for certain groups in
the electorate. Sixty-three percent of those who reported unemployment
to be the most serious national problem reported voting for Carter. This
is almost the exact reverse of the findings for inflation. Also, 58.5 percent
of those *not* reporting unemployment as the most serious problem
supported Mr. Reagan and the Republicans. Thus, the two most frequently
cited economic problems—inflation and unemployment—appear to have
produced effects consistent with an issue-priority model of voting behavior. The "flip-flopping" between issue-priority and reward-punishment models from 1978 to 1980 begins to call into question the utility
of such approaches in the American electoral context and suggests that
a political-debate model of electoral behavior may be more appropriate.
Unemployment and inflation work in favor of Carter and Reagan,
respectively. But as will be shown later, the heightened salience of
inflation produces a more dramatic effect on the election outcome. The
last two issues both worked to the benefit of the Republicans. This was
particularly true of defense (64 percent reporting having voted for Mr.
Reagan) and Iran (53 percent supporting the Republican candidate). The
only surprising result from this analysis is the relatively balanced support
for President Carter and Mr. Reagan on the Iran question.

Table 5.4 shows the bivariate relationship between individual voting
choice in 1972 and partisan preference for specific issues. As was the
case with 1972 and 1976, these bivariate relations show that support

TABLE 5.4 PARTY PREFERRED ON MOST IMPORTANT ISSUES IN 1980
AND PERCENTAGE VOTE FOR CANDIDATES

	Party Preferred		
Issue	Republican %	Undecided* %	Democrat %
Inflation			
Carter	10.2	50.0	95.7
Reagan	89.8	50.0	4.3
N	166	688	23
Iran			
Carter	--**	55.0	93.3
Reagan	100.0	45.0	6.7
N	42	820	15
Unemployment			
Carter	27.3	43.1	100.0
Reagan	72.7	56.9	--**
N	22	840	15
Defense			
Carter	11.8	44.8	100.0
Reagan	88.2	55.2	--**
N	34	840	3

(Total N = 871)

*The "undecided" category includes those who did not mention
a problem, since we assume that those undecided between the
Republican and Democratic parties on an issue behave no
differently than those not citing a problem.

** refers to no cases in cells

for a party on a given issue produces overwhelming electoral support.
For example, of those favoring the Republican approach on inflation,
90 percent voted for Reagan, while those favoring the Democratic
approach on inflation supported Mr. Carter over Ronald Reagan by a
96 to 4 percent margin. However, as already seen, the Republicans were
overwhelmingly favored as the party best able to deal with this issue.
Hence, these data, taken by themselves, can be a bit misleading in
drawing conclusions on the influence of election *outcomes*. They show

rather clearly, though, that at the *individual* level of analysis, party preference on an issue is important in predicting voter behavior. Whether it will prove important in influencing outcomes is still open to question.

As for unemployment, those who favored the Republican position supported Reagan by a 73–27 percent margin, while those who favored the Democratic position on unemployment unanimously supported Mr. Carter. Those favoring the Republican position on Iran and on defense questions voted for Reagan by massive margins of 100 percent and 88 percent, respectively, with similar lopsided results obtaining for those who favored the Democratic approach in their support of Mr. Carter.

The multivariate analyses provide interpretations not dramatically different from the previous findings. Unlike 1976, issues alone, controlling for partisanship, do not exhibit statistically significant effects, although both unemployment and inflation operate in a manner consistent with an issue-priority approach (Table 5.5). That is, those citing unemployment as the most significant problem facing the nation were less likely to vote Republican, other factors being equal, while those citing inflation as the most important problem were more likely to support Mr. Reagan and the Republican party, controlling for other factors. These findings reinforce the earlier findings that the simple "reward-punishment" model of voting behavior does not necessarily always apply (at least in 1980). The question of whether the patterns of support reflect perceptions of stable issue priorities is problematic. What we may be seeing could be a result of the campaign context. Voters in 1980 appeared to respond on the basis of a party's historical performance in a given area, or perhaps what they perceived to be their objective long-term interests. But issue-priority models of political support assume a stability and behavior from one election to the next, a stability that appears to be lacking.

The mediated variables are all statistically significant, as also shown in Table 5.5. Those who supported the Republican approach on unemployment, inflation, Iran, and defense are significantly more likely to vote for Mr. Reagan and the Republicans, even controlling for partisanship. The interesting thing to note in these results is that inflation appears to have had a much stronger effect on voting than on unemployment. This is in contrast to 1976, when unemployment emerged as the dominant problem. Yet, one should remember that in the intervening four years inflation had worsened considerably, while unemployment had declined. Inflation replaced unemployment as the most salient economic issue confronting the electorate and more generally had become the most salient issue overall. The findings further reinforce the view that prospective assessments are important in voting decisions.

TABLE 5.5 PROBIT ESTIMATES OF EFFECTS OF PARTISANSHIP AND
ISSUE-PRIORITY VARIABLES ON 1980 VOTE

Variables	Model One	Model Two
Constant	0.415/(0.105)*	0.176/(0.092)*
Republican Party ID	1.193/(0.160)*	1.164/(0.176)*
Democratic Party ID	-1.161/(0.111)*	-1.633/(0.118)*
Inflation	0.253/(0.190)	1.176/(0.158)*
Unemployment	-0.156/(0.120)	0.956/(0.295)*
Iran	-0.034/(0.161)	1.810/(0.428)*
Defense	0.173/(0.221)	1.192/(0.337)*
(N = 852)		
Estimated R^2	.50	.65
R^2 increment**	.01	.16
Rho	.52	.67
% correctly classified	.79	.82

*$P \leq$ .05

**R^2 increment refers to additional variance explained by the
issue variables over and beyond that explained by partisanship alone.

Individual Voting and the 1980 Election Outcome

The sources of change in the 1980 electorate differed some, but not tremendously, from 1976. Among the potential electorate, 44.2 percent reported supporting the same party over the two elections, a percentage down only from the 47.4 percent seen in 1976. The major difference was in the behavior of switchers. The percentage of switchers as a percentage of the overall electorate was higher—16.4 percent—than in any other election, including the 15.7 percent noted for the Nixon-McGovern race. The percentage of transients, in contrast, shows little fluctuation (Table 5.6).

In a stark reversal of the 1976 election, voting patterns similar to those seen in 1972 are evident when we examine Table 5.7. The introduction to this chapter suggested some of the major forces working

TABLE 5.6   SOURCES OF PERCENT CHANGE IN THE 1976-1980
ELECTIONS

Category	Electorate
Remain[1]	44.2%
Switchers (Major Party)[2]	11.7%
Switchers (Major to Anderson)	4.7%
Transients[3]	6.0%
New Voters[4]	3.7%
Transient and Newly Eligible Nonvoters[5]	10.0%
Nonvoters[6]	19.7%
(Total N = 1,260)	100.0%

[1]Those voting for same party in both 1976 and 1980.

[2]Those who switch from one party candidate to another between
1976 and 1980.

[3]Those voting in 1980 who were eligible to vote in 1976 but
abstained.

[4]Those voting in 1980 who were ineligible to vote in 1976.

[5]Those eligible to vote in 1980 who voted in 1976 but
abstained, and those newly eligible who failed to vote.

[6]Those who failed to vote in both 1976 and 1980.

TABLE 5.7   TURNOVER TABLE, 1976-1980 (1980 VOTING PATTERNS BY
1976 VOTING PATTERNS)

	1976 Vote			
1980 Vote	Ford	Carter	Non Voter	Ineligible
Reagan	74.4	23.4	11.8	21.0
Carter	10.2	56.7	9.6	23.5
Anderson	6.9	7.1	1.9	12.3
Abstained	8.4	12.8	76.8	43.2
(Total N = 1,260)	403.0	453.0	323.0	81.0

chi-square = 827.31   d.f. = 9,   p < .001

Cramer's V = .46

against Mr. Carter's 1980 reelection effort. Mr. Reagan was able to improve significantly upon President Ford's ability to retain Republican voters from the previous election. As will be recalled, Mr. Ford was only able to attract 66 percent of those who had supported Richard Nixon in 1972. In contrast, Ronald Reagan managed to improve upon this performance by 8 points, attracting 74 percent of the voters who had supported Gerald Ford four years earlier. This is somewhat surprising, particularly given the bitter nomination struggle which had been fought by Ford and Reagan during the 1976 primary season and convention.

In addition, while Ford had suffered the loss of a full 23 percent of former Nixon supporters defecting to Mr. Carter, Reagan had to contend with only 10 percent of Ford supporters defecting to President Carter. In fact, almost as many former Ford supporters defected to Congressman John Anderson, the third party candidate, as supported Mr. Carter. Seven percent of Ford voters reported ultimately voting for Anderson.

The picture for the Democrats was, in contrast, quite gloomy. About 23 percent of Carter voters defected to the Republican candidate in 1980, a figure not markedly lower than the 28 percent of 1968 Humphrey supporters who had abandoned George McGovern and the Democrats in 1972 to support the Republican ticket.

The Michigan surveys suggest that almost precisely the same (7 percent) proportion of Carter supporters in 1976 abandoned the 1980 Democratic nominee to support Mr. Anderson, as was the case with the Republicans. Nonetheless, this does not necessarily suggest that Anderson's candidacy had a totally neutralizing effect on the major party candidates. Given Anderson's relatively liberal stands on social issues and certain economic concerns, it appears logical to conclude that perhaps a majority of the Anderson vote would have gone to Carter in a two-man race. Obviously, however, this could not have substantively influenced the actual election outcome. Few other surprises were revealed by the turnover table. While 77 percent of all 1976 nonvoters again abstained in 1980, those who did vote favored Reagan with 50 percent of the vote, with 42 percent supporting Mr. Carter, and 8 percent voting for the independent John Anderson.

Among the newly eligible voters, a rather large proportion (43 percent) acknowledged not voting, with the rest distributing their vote in a fashion which gave Carter 42 percent of the vote, with Reagan and Anderson receiving 37 and 21 percent of the vote, respectively. Anderson clearly was quite attractive to the younger, newly eligible voters, though the Democrats, as had been historically the case, continued to do quite well among this group. It should be remembered that, of the three elections so far examined, the best performance by a Republican candidate was in 1972, although even in this case Mr. Nixon was able to secure only one-half of this group's support.

Issues and the 1980 Election Outcome

The aggregate-level analysis of the 1980 election would not be complete without examining the effects of specific issues on the actual election outcome. By now one should be reasonably familiar with the pattern of shifting from one election to another on various issues and within various groups. While in 1972 all issues worked uniformly in favor of Mr. Nixon—albeit with widely different impacts on the net vote—1976 produced a much more complex pattern, with no single candidate benefitting across all categories of voters or issues.

The 1980 election analysis is similar to 1976 to the extent that economic issues appear to have played a crucial role in the outcome, but similar to 1972 in that one candidate—Mr. Reagan—for the most part outperformed incumbent President Jimmy Carter on most issues and among the electoral categories. More importantly, 1980 differed dramatically from 1972 in that a single issue—in this case, inflation—was so highly salient and, hence, had an opportunity to produce large aggregate effects because it unidirectionally favored the Republicans.

Inflation was the single most important issue, mentioned by 32 percent of all those citing a problem. Inflation was also clearly important in our bivariate analyses, and at least approached statistical significance in the multivariate probits. Inflation was—as will be shown—to Jimmy Carter in 1980 what unemployment had been in 1976 for Gerald R. Ford. Reagan was favored on the inflation issue by all three categories of voters, doing best among the loyalists where he outpaced the Georgian by 61–39 percent. Crucial, however, was the fact that inflation resulted in a net vote gain for Mr. Reagan of a full 9 percentage points, similar to the net gain Carter had won over the unemployment question four years earlier (Table 5.8). Nearly 3 percent of this gain came from those switching to the Republicans.

In contrast to 1976, unemployment had dropped to only third as the most important single issue. Still, like 1976 but to a lesser extent, unemployment worked to the benefit of the Democrats. President Carter was favored by the loyalists and by the new-transient voter group, winning with margins of 64 and 73 percent, respectively. One odd note, though, was independent John Anderson's ability to attract 48 percent of the switchers on the unemployment issue. This may well have reflected the depth of despair of at least some Democrats and liberal Republicans, given the options offered by the two major parties, but probably in particular reflected the disillusionment of some former Carter supporters.

TABLE 5.8 EFFECT OF ISSUES IN THE 1980
PRESIDENTIAL ELECTION*

	1980 Vote		
Voting Pattern	Reagan	Carter	Anderson
Inflation			
Switch (N = 207)	53 (4.4)	18 (1.5)	29 (2.0)
Remain (N = 557)	61(13.6)	39 (8.5)	0 (---)[a]
Enter/Reenter (N = 121)	52 (2.0)	38 (1.2)	10 (0.3)
	20.0	11.2	2.3
Iran			
Switch (N = 207)	59 (1.0)	23 (0.4)	18 (0.3)
Remain (N = 557)	51 (4.7)	49 (4.5)	-- (---)
Enter/Reenter (N = 121)	50 (1.5)	33 (1.0)	17 (0.5)
	7.2	6.0	0.8
Unemployment			
Switch (N = 207)	19 (0.4)	33 (0.7)	48 (1.0)
Remain (N = 557)	36 (1.9)	64 (3.3)	-- (---)
Enter/Reenter (N = 121)	27 (0.4)	73 (1.2)	-- (---)
	2.7	5.2	1.0
Defense			
Switch (N = 207)	47 (1.0)	37 (0.8)	16 (0.3)
Remain (N = 557)	68 (2.1)	21 (0.9)	-- (---)
Enter/Reenter (N = 121)	71 (0.4)	19 (0.1)	-- (---)
	3.5	1.8	0.3

(Total N = 885)

*Figures not in parentheses represent percentage support for
candidate; figures in parentheses are vote as percentage of
entire electorate.

[a]Less than .1 percent, or empty cell

Yet overall, Carter benefitted from this issue with a net advantage of
2.5 percent of the vote. This clearly was insufficient to offset the damage
done by the preeminent issue of rising prices. While the Carter margin
on unemployment may have been quite handsome, the decline in salience
of this issue assured that Mr. Carter could not count on it to produce
the kind of dramatic electoral effects seen in 1976.

The issues of Iran and defense produced relatively little change in
the outcome. The Iranian issue, despite all the publicity associated with
it, seems to have changed less than 2 percent of the actual vote in
Reagan's favor. The question of defense and military preparedness seems
to have produced a similar effect, providing Reagan with a modest 1.5
percent of the votes, in spite of the relatively high level of support

Reagan had on these issues. Had these issues been more salient, Reagan would have probably achieved an even larger margin of victory.

While Carter may have been damaged by the relative lack of salience of unemployment, Reagan's margin was restrained by the relatively modest visibility of Iran and defense. Hence, although Reagan was favored over Carter on the Iran issue by margins of 59–23 percent among switchers, and 50–33 percent among the new and transient voters, these groups did not comprise a sufficiently large proportion of the total electorate to make a difference on the outcome. And the narrow 51–49 percent pro-Reagan margin among loyalists was a "wash," producing little aggregate effect.

Defense and military preparedness saw a similar pattern. While Reagan drew consistently heavy support among switchers, loyalists, and new-transient voters, the low salience contributed to the extremely modest 1.7 percent overall vote gain for Mr. Reagan.

These findings clearly suggest that, as in 1976, economic issues were the key to determining the election outcome. Unlike 1976, though, one does not observe a tendency for various issues to exhibit a cross-cutting effect in which electoral gains on one issue are "washed out" by losses on other issues. With the exception of unemployment, all issues worked in Reagan's favor, even though two issues—Iran and defense—do not appear to have had massive effects. The overall influence of these four issues produced a net vote effect of approximately 8.5 percent, with about 4 percent being accounted for by switchers.

The results shown in Table 5.9 reveal little that is different from the basic examination of issue responses and voting patterns in the previous section. Inflation remained far and away the single most important determinant of the 1980 election outcome, producing a net pro-Republican effect of nearly 12 percentage points. This is remarkably similar to the results obtained in the previous section. Most impressive is that the Republicans clearly dominated among the switchers, even though, as one would expect, the total effect of this group was not quite so high as for those who stayed with the Republicans between 1976 and 1980. Still, virtually none of the Carter vote could be accounted for by switchers on the inflation issue; 3 percent of the Reagan vote, in contrast, was due to this issue. Reagan also achieved a massive 9 point vote gain among the loyalists.

Among those undecided on the issue of inflation, Reagan was favored only slightly. Unemployment worked in favor of Carter, but as with inflation in 1976, the effects were relatively trivial. The aggregate, net effect of the two dominant economic issues was approximately 10.5 percent in favor of Mr. Reagan and the Republicans. The Iranian hostage issue and the question of defense also appear to have played some role,

TABLE 5.9   INFLUENCE OF PARTY PREFERRED ON ISSUES IN THE 1980 PRESIDENTIAL ELECTION*

		1980 Vote		
Voting Pattern	Reagan	Undecided[a] Reagan	Carter	Carter
Inflation				
Switch (N = 207)	3.0	9.0	4.1	---[b]
Remain (N = 557)	11.0	22.6	25.5	2.2
Enter/Reenter (N = 121)	---	4.7	5.1	---
	14.0	36.3	34.6	2.2
Iran				
Switch (N = 207)	0.9	11.0	4.5	0.1
Remain (N = 557)	2.6	31.0	27.8	1.2
Enter/Reenter (N = 121)	1.0	5.2	5.6	---
	4.5	47.2	37.9	1.3
Unemployment				
Switch (N = 207)	0.1	11.9	4.4	---
Remain (N = 557)	1.2	32.6	26.9	1.6
Enter/Reenter (N = 121)	0.2	5.8	4.9	0.6
	1.5	50.3	36.2	2.2
Defense				
Switch (N = 207)	0.8	11.1	4.2	0.1
Remain (N = 557)	1.7	32.2	28.7	0.1
Enter/Reenter (N = 121)	0.5	5.6	5.5	0.1
	3.0	48.9	38.4	0.3

(Total N = 885)

*Figures are as a percent of the total electorate. See text for further explanation.

[a]Undecided category includes those not citing a problem as "most important" or citing problems other than those under study.

[b]Less than .1 percent, or empty cell

as the analysis of the previous section suggests. Indeed, in both cases they have a slightly stronger effect—albeit in a Republican direction— than unemployment had in a Democratic direction. "Iran" and "defense" produced, respectively, net gains for the Republicans of about 3.2 and 2.7 percent, which were certainly modest, but not trivial by any means.

Summary

Any effort to synthesize the individual and aggregate-level findings for the 1980 election must include reference to the analysis of the 1976 election. It will be recalled that unemployment was shown to be the single most important issue at the individual level, as well as the one issue which most clearly influenced the actual election outcome. With regard to the individual-level analysis, the findings suggest that a simple reward-punishment model, in which voters decide whether the governing party meets some particular subjective criterion of economic performance, seemed evident.

Further, the one issue which clearly dominated the individual-level analysis also produced the largest pro-Democratic shift at the aggregate level in creating a Democratic victory. In the same vein, the analysis of individual voting behavior can be seen as providing at least some evidence for a policy-oriented response of the electorate in 1980, given the fact that, once again, unemployment is *negatively* related to voting Republican, while inflation is *positively* related to support for the Republican candidate. At the aggregate level, the size effects of unemployment and inflation are reversed, for in 1980 inflation was the one issue which dominated the electoral landscape, providing massive Republican gains. The reduced salience of unemployment, together with a weakening—though not disappearance—of the party link of unemployment to the Democrats, served to reduce the net effect. To the extent that a mandate existed in the 1980 election, though, it was to deal with the inflationary spiral.

Iran and the hostage crisis certainly had potential to do even greater harm to the Democrats than it in fact did. Iran, however, was a "dangerous" issue and one downplayed by Reagan during the campaign, possibly from concern for an "October surprise" which could have brought about the release of the hostages, thus rebounding against him. These concerns, plus possible concern that criticisms of the President on the issue could backfire and force Reagan to spell out his own position, at least partially neutralized it as an issue.

The defense question, a classical example of a positional issue, also worked—though not dramatically—in Reagan's favor. Carter had allowed himself to be pinned in a relatively weak position and was unable to convince the electorate that his solutions were superior to those of his Republican opponent.

Do these findings inform us as to the existence of a mandate in 1980? As in 1976, only one issue, inflation, was decisive in explaining the election outcome. While it appears likely that the dynamics of the campaign influenced the impact of issues on electoral behavior, from what has been suggested as a "campaign debate" model—the presence, albeit temporary, of a prospective component to the electorate's decisionmaking—there may indeed have existed a kind of mandate not present four years earlier. Voters may not simply have been punishing the incumbent (although performance assessments of the incumbent were assuredly important), but might have been signalling a willingness to accept certain policies historically associated with Republicans to bring inflation under control. Still, Reagan himself appears to have done little to indicate explicit policies he would follow if elected. Of course, an alternative interpretation would be that those concerned with inflation were punishing Carter for his performance, while those concerned with unemployment based their decision on an assessment of the future consequences of voting for Reagan, even if they were dissatisfied with the incumbent. Even if this were the case, however, the transient nature of voter support for parties on issues would in all likelihood make an administration hesitant to follow through with long-term policies. If voter support is so transient, parties and political leaders would see themselves as foolhardy in taking any action which would jeopardize their bases of support.

6

The 1984 Election: 1972 Replayed?

In the 1984 U.S. presidential election, Ronald Reagan defeated Democratic nominee Walter Mondale by an overwhelming margin of 59 to 41 percent. Former Vice-President Mondale suffered the ignominy of carrying only his home state of Minnesota and the District of Columbia. Mondale had the great misfortune of running against an extraordinarily popular political figure who was widely perceived as being strong and decisive, in addition to communicating a sunny, optimistic view of the world.[1]

Although one might argue whether the 1984 election results represented a policy mandate for the Reagan administration, it most emphatically did not provide any solace for those looking for signs of a revival of the New Deal coalition. The group alignments evident in the 1984 presidential voting represented an extraordinary shift from those of the New Deal era. In particular, major shifts were evident among working class and Catholic voters, with only blacks more firmly entrenched in the Democratic camp.[2] While there was evidence of shifts in group loyalties at the presidential level, uncertainty remained concerning whether the electorate was experiencing an actual long-term partisan realignment.[3] Although Republicans had won four of the last five presidential elections, the Democratic party was still quite strong in Congress and at the state and local levels. In addition, there was no firm evidence of a permanent shift in partisan identification. Measures of partisanship undergo some seasonal fluctuations and are partially captive to short-term events. Still, Democratic partisan identification had been maintained, though with some slippage from the 1960s. In August of 1984, 42 percent of the electorate identified with the Democrats, 28 percent identified with the Republicans, and 22 percent classified themselves as independents. Exit polls conducted by the networks at the time of the November elections seemed to represent, in Nelson Polsby's view, a "blip" for the Republicans. From the Republican viewpoint, the most optimistic survey was NBC's, which showed the two parties in a dead heat with a 32–32 percent tie in identification. But, by January 1985, Democratic identification had rebounded somewhat, with the Democrats holding a 49–45 percent lead among registered voters.[4] These findings reflect the view that partisanship is an endogenous variable, subject to a variety of "shocks." In general, most evidence seems to suggest that realignment has taken place at the *presidential* level but not at lower levels or at the level of partisan identification.[5] Even given these provisions and qualifications, 1984 was important for what we did *not* see; i.e., the reassertion of traditional voting patterns. By "traditional voting patterns," I refer to the historic tendency of blue-collar, labor, and a variety of white-ethnic voters to support the Democratic party. This clearly did not occur in 1984, nor in 1980. Thus, we should ask how the Republicans and Reagan managed this outcome and what the Democratic party did (or did not do) which contributed to its electoral defeat. Certainly, one rather parsimonious response to this question is that it is difficult to oust any incumbent president when the nation is at peace, when the electorate perceives that the economy is performing well, and when there are no major "shocks" to the system.[6] Still, the outcome was not pre-ordained.

Through much of 1981, President Reagan had dominated the political arena, achieving important congressional victories with domestic budget cuts and tax reductions, in addition to increases in defense spending in an effort to redress what he saw as the nation's dangerous decline in military preparedness. By May of that year, the president's overall popularity rating was 68 percent, an 8 point gain over the pre-assassination attempt level.[7] Figure 6.1 plots Reagan's popularity during his first term.[8] As with Chapters 3 through 5, Figure 6.2 plots the unemployment and inflation rates for the same period.[9] In addition, Reagan drew strong approval in specific policy areas, including national defense (62 percent) and inflation (58 percent). Only regarding unemployment, with an approval rating of just 42 percent, was he lagging. As events would show, Reagan's popularity was closely associated with the state of the economy. From the May high of 68 percent, his popularity declined to 47 percent by the end of the first year and to 35 percent by the end of the second year. Unemployment rose steadily during this period and reached a high of 10.6 percent in December 1982—the highest level of joblessness since the Great Depression of the 1930s.[10] The perception of unemployment as the nation's most important problem increased quickly; in January of 1982, 49 percent of the public considered *inflation* the chief problem, with only 28 percent citing unemployment. Within three months, those concerns were virtually reversed with unemployment ahead 44–24 percent.[11]

Reagan's political fortunes were not quite as bleak as these figures would suggest. The inflation rate was declining rapidly during this early period. From a 12 percent annual rate, inflation declined to 6 percent

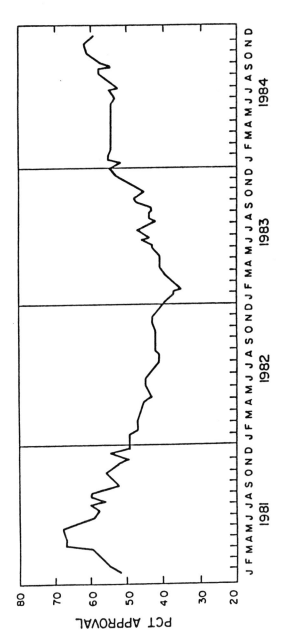

Figure 6.1.   Trend in Reagan Gallup Approval Rating, 1981-1984

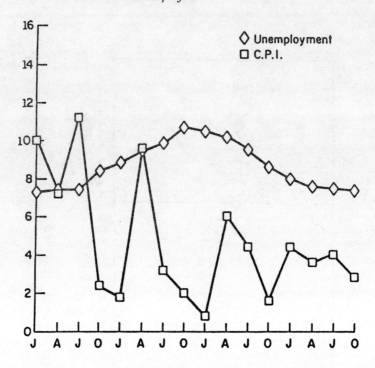

◇ Unemployment
□ C.P.I.

Figure 6.2.   Trends in Inflation and Unemployment,   1981-1984

for 1982 and would drop even further in 1983 and 1984. At the same time, the increase in unemployment and concomitant decline in growth reduced tax revenues, leading to massive increases in the federal budget deficit. As Ranney,[12] Chubb and Peterson,[13] and others have noted, this produced an interesting shift in traditional party positions, with the Republicans downplaying the potentially pernicious impact of the deficit and the Democrats dramatizing its effects. However, the nation began to climb out of the recession by early 1983. Along with the economic recovery, Reagan's popularity rating also recovered. By the summer of 1983, his monthly approval levels were back into the mid-40 percent range and continued a fairly steady rise.[14]

Although the economy remained the single most important issue, Reagan gave the "social issues" of abortion and school prayer somewhat more attention in 1982 and 1983, but his support generally did not extend far beyond formal endorsements of particular positions advocated by conservative activists.[15] Foreign affairs and foreign policy also became more visible. There were several controversies, but certainly one major administration success in late 1983 was the deployment of U.S. intermediate range missiles in Western Europe, in spite of a massive Soviet propaganda campaign to block deployment. The destruction of a South Korean airliner by the Soviets also made Soviet-American relations more visible and salient. Other salient foreign policy areas included the character of American involvement in El Salvador and Nicaragua. While Reagan's anti-communist rhetoric was criticized by liberals, his policies were basically cautious and pragmatic.

Two major events in October 1983 also served to focus attention on foreign policy. The deaths of over 200 American marines in Lebanon, resulting from a terrorist attack, seemed to demonstrate the inadequacy of administration policy and strategy in that part of the world. The Grenada intervention, justified by the President on grounds of rescuing American students, as well as protecting the Caribbean from the expansion of Cuban and Soviet influence, served to differentiate the forceful stands taken by this president from the perceived weakness and incompetence of Jimmy Carter.

Although Reagan entered 1984 in a strong position, there was no shortage of Democratic contenders. The acknowledged front runner, Walter Mondale, was attempting to pull together the traditional New Deal coalition of labor, blacks, ethnic groups, and liberals. Mondale had considerable national political experience as a senator and later as Jimmy Carter's vice-president, but he was viewed by many, within and outside of the party, as wedded to the Democratic liberalism of the past. Senators Gary Hart and John Glenn, for example, attacked Mondale by suggesting the party needed to move beyond the New Dealism which had proved successful in the past, but which was inadequate to assure political success in the present era.[16]

In 1984, early surveys showed Mondale and Glenn running close races with Reagan. These results contrasted sharply with surveys taken in 1982 which had shown both Mondale and Hart defeating the president by rather substantial margins of 10–15 points.[17] Hart, consistently emphasizing the twin themes of "new leadership" and "new ideas," managed to surprise many with his showing in the Iowa caucus. He then proceeded to defeat Mondale in New Hampshire. Subsequently, the former vice-president managed to survive the "Super Tuesday" primaries in the South and went on to win several primaries in the Midwest and industrial Northeast. The latter effectively clinched the nomination, although Hart did make a partial comeback in the last wave of primaries held in the West in May and June. At the party's July convention in San Francisco, Mondale received his party's nomination on the first ballot.

Entering the fall campaign, the Democrats faced an uphill struggle. Although they had briefly drawn even with the Republicans in surveys taken immediately after the convention, Reagan and the Republicans soon rebounded with Reagan taking a 10-point lead in a Gallup survey taken in August. Surely one reason for the transient nature of the Democratic recovery involved the intense, albeit temporary, media attention surrounding any convention.[18] Also, the dramatic speeches of Governor Mario Cuomo and the Reverend Jesse Jackson, both well received by the party, had briefly served to draw attention away from the divisive struggle for the nomination.[19]

In addition, Mondale's selection of Geraldine Ferraro had generated generally favorable public reaction and served to diminish charges that the Democratic presidential nominee was excessively cautious and orthodox. The Ferraro candidacy also temporarily highlighted what the media had dubbed the "gender gap." This phenomenon had first appeared in 1980, when pollsters noted that, while Reagan had outpolled Carter by an almost 2 to 1 margin among men, he had only managed to break even among women.[20] Thus, there appeared to be some potential for the Democrats to take advantage of an apparent perception among many women that the Democratic party better represented their interests, given the Republicans' opposition to the Equal Rights Amendment, abortion, and other gender-related issues. Unfortunately for the Democrats, the controversy surrounding Ferraro and her husband's finances served to tarnish the candidacy of the first woman vice-presidential candidate. Soon after the beginning of the fall campaign, Elizabeth Drew noted, there were some who thought the Ferraro candidacy was as much a burden as an advantage to the Democratic ticket.[21]

Regarding campaign issues, Mondale had consistently denounced the budget deficit throughout the primary campaign and continued this line of attack following the conventions. One of his more controversial proposals made at the convention, in fact, was a declaration that he would raise taxes, if elected, in order to balance the deficit. He also charged that Reagan was not being forthright about what he would do if reelected. While this may have allowed Mondale to score points for his political honesty, it made him vulnerable to the charge that this merely represented the philosophy of "tax and tax, spend and spend."[22] Reagan also had partially insulated himself from being damaged by the deficit issue through his consistent support of a balanced budget amendment and his frequent criticism of Congress for failing to reduce adequately social expenditures. As the campaign progressed, it was not at all clear that the Democrats would benefit from the deficit issue.[23]

Other economic issues at best played a subsidiary role in the campaign. Although unemployment hovered at 7 percent, the Democratic strategy of attempting to mute some of its more traditional impulses prevented any calls for public employment programs because of the effect of such expenditures on the deficit. The major Democratic plan for dealing with unemployment was to do so indirectly through reducing the budget deficit, which would in turn reduce interest rates and hence stimulate economic growth. This was clearly a calculated tradeoff. By intentionally reducing the salience of unemployment, they hoped to attract more middle class support which would compensate for any working class disaffection.

Other issues never really seemed to capture the attention or imagination of voters. The early weeks of the campaign had seen the question of church-state relations and questions involving the proper role of religion in civil society. This debate was complicated by criticisms by the Catholic Archbishop of New York, John O'Connor, and Geraldine Ferraro when Ferraro accused the Archbishop of using his official position in the Church hierarchy to criticize her pro-choice position on abortion. Some of these developments also may have served to direct attention away from the close ties the Republicans had developed with fundamentalist Christian groups such as Jerry Falwell's Moral Majority.[24]

Although social issues may have been salient to some voters, they do not appear to have had any wide-ranging impact on the election. Going into October, the only chance left to the Democrats appeared to rest with the debates. Surveys showed Reagan with massive leads of from 20 to 25 points. The first debate in Louisville on October 7 provided Mondale with some temporary impetus and, for a brief time, a new issue. Reagan's faltering performance, in contrast to Mondale's clear command of the issues, resulted in the surfacing of the age issue. Although polls showed it never became an overriding concern of the public, it was a potential point of vulnerability for the president. This issue tended to frame the second debate in Kansas City on October 21. Although Reagan still appeared halting at times, his performance was sufficiently improved to reassure voters that he was still in command.[25]

The last two weeks of the campaign were anti-climactic. Reagan's support, which had declined slightly during the interval between the debates, solidified and actually increased once again. Although in this, as in virtually every election, there were disclaimers that the polls were wrong, the outcome on November 6 showed conclusively that for the most part the pre-election surveys had been quite accurate. Reagan captured an overwhelming popular and electoral vote majority, winning in every region and decimating Mondale in the South which, since 1952, had (with the exception of Carter in 1976) become increasingly Republican at the presidential level.

After each election, the question is raised whether realignment has occurred. As with the 1980 election, it is still too early to tell. Clearly, there does appear to be a shift in certain group voting patterns which

TABLE 6.1   MOST IMPORTANT ISSUES IN 1984

Issue	N	Percentage Mentioning Problem as "Most Important"*	
		(1)	(2)
Budget Deficit	333	17.1	18.3
Unemployment	278	14.3	15.8
War Fear	272	14.0	15.3

N is the number of respondents.

*Column (1) includes all respondents whether or not they cited a problem as most important.   Column (2) includes only those mentioning a problem.

would be part of a general realignment, at least at the presidential level.[26] The question of a possibly enduring realignment aside, it seems clear that the 1984 results were due to two overriding factors: first, the genuinely positive orientation and even affection that a majority of Americans expressed toward the president and, second, the general satisfaction of a majority of voters with the way things were going, either for themselves or for the country. Quite simply, the fact that the country was at peace and in a period of relative prosperity created a very favorable climate for the incumbent president.

Individual Voting Behavior in 1984

Viewed in comparative perspective, the 1984 election again demonstrates the dynamic nature of the issues which concern the American electorate. The three most frequently mentioned problems (Table 6.1) were the budget deficit, unemployment, and concern about possible U.S. military involvement. The last issue, abbreviated "war fear," consists of two types of responses: fear of U.S. involvement in a conventional or Vietnam-type war and, second, fear of a nuclear conflict between the U.S. and the Soviet Union.

This set of issues represents a sharp break with 1980, when the most important issues cited by the CPS election survey respondents were inflation, unemployment, Iran, and defense spending. Unemployment thereby was the only top priority issue remaining from 1980, and there was no other single issue cited as most important (using the general criterion of 5 percent). Inflation, which was the single most important problem in 1980, had virtually disappeared as an issue, being cited by only 4 percent of respondents (and hence not included in the analysis). Unemployment, relatively high by post-war standards and at approximately the same levels as in November of 1980, was highlighted as a result of the lingering effects of the severe recession of 1981–82, which had seen unemployment climb to the highest level since the 1930s. Unemployment was mentioned by 14 percent of all respondents, and 16 percent of those actually mentioned a problem. Finally, the budget deficit and "war fear" were newcomers on the issue agenda. Both would appear, at first glance, to have valence-type properties. However, no single issue appeared salient to sufficient numbers of voters to affect significantly the election outcome.

When issue-party ties are examined, one finds that only on the budget deficit, which appeared as the single most salient issue, were Mr. Reagan and the Republicans favored (see Table 6.2). Thirty-seven percent believed the GOP was most capable of dealing with the deficit; 23 percent favored the Democrats and 43 percent were undecided. These findings are ironic, given Mondale's strategy of emphasizing the problems which could arise in the future as a result of the deficit, and his attempt to link these to Reagan's policies and performance. They suggest that the Democrats would have fared better had they downplayed, rather than emphasized, the deficit.

The other issues, "war fear" and unemployment, seemed to work to the benefit of the Democrats, although the findings for unemployment were somewhat surprising, given that unemployment was higher than during the 1976 election when the Democrats possessed an overwhelming advantage on that issue. Yet, the salience of unemployment was reduced by 1984. Further, the salience, as well as the link to the Democrats, was probably reduced by the favorable trends in unemployment since early 1983, given that it had fallen from more than 10.5 percent to its November level of 7.5 percent.

Regarding actual voting behavior, Table 6.3 shows that majorities who cited an issue as "most important" supported Mr. Reagan and the Republicans in each instance. As for the most frequently mentioned problem, the budget deficit, the analysis suggests that this issue actually worked in favor of Mr. Reagan and the Republicans. Indeed, there was a 7 percent pro-Republican advantage for those *mentioning* this issue as opposed to those *not mentioning* it. Whereas Reagan was favored by a 64–36 margin among those mentioning the budget deficit as being most important, Reagan carried only 57 percent of the vote among those *not* citing the deficit as most important.

TABLE 6.2   PARTY PREFERRED IN 1984 ON MOST IMPORTANT ISSUES*

Issue	Republican N %	Undecided N %	Democrat N %
Budget Deficit	124 (37.2)	142 (42.6)	67 (20.1)
Unemployment	59 (21.2)	131 (47.1)	88 (31.6)
War Fear	69 (25.3)	127 (46.6)	76 (27.9)

N in each category is the number of respondents citing the party as best able to handle that particular issue. Numbers in parentheses are the percentages favoring that party on a particular issue.

TABLE 6.3   REPORTED PERCENTAGE VOTE FOR CANDIDATES IN 1984 BY SELECTED MOST IMPORTANT ISSUES

Candidate	Budget Deficit NM M	Unemployment NM M	War Fear NM M
Mondale	43.1 35.8	40.3 49.2	40.4 48.4
Reagan	56.9 64.2	59.7 50.8	59.6 51.6
(Total N = 1,327)	1,042.0 285.0	1,142.0 185.0	1,135.0 192.0

- NM refers to those respondents <u>not mentioning</u> a problem as most important.

- M refers to those respondents <u>mentioning</u> a particular issue as most important.

NOTE: Percentages have been rounded to the nearest one-tenth percent.

Very small majorities of those naming unemployment and "war fear" as the major problems also supported Mr. Reagan, who attained support levels of 52 and 51 percent, respectively, among those mentioning those issues. However, 60 percent of those *not mentioning* those issues voted for Reagan. This suggests that unemployment and fear of military involvement may actually have worked marginally against the president. The results on the unemployment issue contrast sharply with 1980, when 63 percent of those identifying unemployment as the chief problem reported voting for Jimmy Carter. Still, where there may have been a weakening of the relationship between unemployment and support for the Democratic party, that relationship did not disappear. Those identifying unemployment as most important were still more likely to vote

TABLE 6.4   PARTY PREFERRED ON MOST IMPORTANT ISSUES IN 1984
AND PERCENTAGE VOTE FOR CANDIDATES

| | Party Preferred | | |
Issue	Republican %	Undecided* %	Democrat %
Budget Deficit			
Mondale	3.6	42.4	95.1
Reagan	96.4	57.6	4.9
N	110.0	1,156.0	61.0
Unemployment			
Mondale	9.3	40.4	90.3
Reagan	90.7	59.6	9.7
N	43.0	1,222.0	62.0
War Fear			
Mondale	7.5	40.9	89.5
Reagan	92.5	59.1	10.5
N	53.0	1,216.0	57.0

*The "undecided" category includes those who did not mention
a problem, since we assume that those undecided between the
Republican and Democratic parties on an issue behave no
differently than those not citing a problem.

for Democratic candidates. These analyses suggest that none of the issues
examined acted in a fashion characteristic of valence issues. Of the three
noted, unemployment and budget deficit would certainly be identified
as valence in nature, yet they failed to work against the incumbent as
would be suggested by their designation as valence issues. In the case
of the deficit, Reagan had been able to defuse this issue by not only
blaming Congress, but by stressing the Democratic "solution" to the
problem through higher taxes; hence, a valence issue became transformed
into a positional issue through clever strategy.

The findings shown in Table 6.4 are typical of those presented in
Chapters 3 through 5. Support for a party on a particular issue was
overwhelmingly associated with votes for that party. Ninety-six percent
of those supporting the Republican position on the budget deficit voted
for Reagan, with comparable percentages voting for Mondale. Similar
results were seen for "war fear" and unemployment. In each case, support

TABLE 6.5   PROBIT ESTIMATES OF EFFECTS OF PARTISANSHIP AND
ISSUE-PRIORITY VARIABLES ON 1984 VOTE

Variables	Model One	Model Two
Constant	0.519/(0.084)*	0.486/(0.076)*
Republican Party ID	1.245/(0.131)*	1.157/(0.139)*
Democratic Party ID	-1.288/(0.095)*	-1.173/(0.101)*
Budget Deficit	-0.006/(0.110)	1.581/(0.216)*
Unemployment	0.028/(0.126)	0.902/(0.190)*
War Fear	-0.118/(0.126)	1.060/(0.194)*
(N = 1,284)		
Estimated R^2	.54	.66
R^2 increment**	.01	.13
Rho	.52	.56
% correctly classified	.79	.84

*$P \leq$ .05

**R^2 increment refers to additional variance explained by the
issue variables over and beyond that explained by partisanship alone.

for a party on an issue produced 90–92 percent support for the candidate
at the polls.

The multivariate analyses basically confirm the results of the tabular
analyses. When the effect of issues alone (controlling for partisanship)
are examined, concern with the budget deficit and military involvement
were marginally related to a propensity to vote Democratic (Table 6.5).
However, none of the coefficients for these issues was close to being
statistically significant. The trivial impact of unemployment really does
not allow for a discussion of reward-punishment versus issue-priority
model of voting. In contrast, as in previous elections, the mediated
issue-party variables produced very respectable results. As in the 1972,
1976, and 1980 elections, support for the Republican party position on
issues was strongly and significantly related to votes for the Republican
party, with the budget deficit having the strongest impact. To recapitulate,
when individuals are capable of identifying a party which they believe

best able to handle that problem, then issues emerge as a significant influence on the vote. Again, these findings illustrate the consistent importance of prospective voting across all four presidential elections. In 1984, all three mediated variables—i.e., those for the budget, war fear, and unemployment—were statistically significant, with concern over the budget deficit having the strongest impact.

The efficacy of the two models also can be compared in terms of the variance explained by the respective variables each included. The first explains a rather healthy 54 percent of the variance, but issues explain only one percent of the total. In contrast, the latter explains fully 66 percent of the variance, of which 13 percent is accounted for by the mediated variables.

Individual Voting and the 1984 Election Outcome

Unfortunately for a study of the 1984 election, the traditional CPS survey question asking how the respondent voted in the 1980 election was omitted from the 1984 survey. Since the previous vote is not known, an effort was made to find a surrogate variable which might at least partially replace it. Partisan identification was one possibility. As noted in previous chapters, partisan identification is an important factor in explaining individual-level electoral behavior. Sometimes, however, short-term forces such as issues or candidate orientations may dampen the psychological attachment to a political party, thus leading the individual to vote against his partisan preference. Converse,[27] in fact, had introduced the concept of the "normal vote," whereby the electoral decision is based entirely on long-term partisan forces, i.e., the electorate votes their party identifications.

But, in reality, as just noted, short-term influences impinge upon these long-term partisan forces operating upon the electorate. Electoral outcomes are dramatically affected by the tendency of partisan identifiers of one party to "cross over" and vote for another party. In 1972, for example, it is clear from Table 6.6 that Mr. Nixon did extremely well in holding Republican identifiers. Indeed, Republicans who voted for Senator McGovern constituted only 1.8 percent of the total electorate, while Democratic party identifiers voting for Mr. Nixon constituted a massive 17.2 percent of the electorate. Obviously, certain short-term forces were at work pulling Democratic identifiers away from the Democratic candidate. As Chapter 2 suggests, issues played a role in this process.

The 1976 election, in contrast, seemed to come fairly close to Converse's normal vote model. The percentage of the electorate who were "switchers," i.e., those partisan identifiers who voted *against* their identification was

TABLE 6.6   PARTISAN IDENTIFICATION AND VOTING BEHAVIOR AS A
PERCENTAGE OF TOTAL ELECTORATE, 1972-1984

Voting Pattern*	1972	1976	1980	1984
Republicans Voting Republican	27.2	24.5	24.5	31.4
Republicans Voting Democratic	1.8	3.6	1.3	1.5
Independents Voting Republican	19.9	17.8	17.9	18.5
Independents Voting Democratic	10.1	14.5	8.5	8.0
Democrats Voting Republican	17.2	7.1	9.1	8.5
Democrats Voting Democratic	23.9	32.4	30.2	32.2
(Total N =	1,559.0	1,305.0	871.0	1,327.0)
Republican-Democratic Differential**	-15.4	-3.5	-7.8	-7.0

*Republicans and Democrats are classified as those who
identify themselves as Strong or Weak Republicans or
Democrats on the standard CPS 7 point scale.   Independents
include "pure" Independents as well as the independent
"leaners," i.e., Independent Republicans and Independent
Democrats.

**The Republican-Democratic differential is calculated by
subtracting the percentage of those Repubicans voting
Democratic from the Democrats voting Republican.

quite low; some 3.6 percent of the electorate were Republicans voting
for Carter, and 7.1 percent were Democrats voting for Ford (Table 6.6).
The years 1980 and 1984, however, resemble 1972. In the former (where
for ease of presentational purposes the Anderson vote has been excluded),
Republicans voting for Carter constituted only 1.3 percent of the overall
electorate, whereas Democrats voting for Reagan constituted 9.1 percent.
In 1984, somewhat similar results obtained.

   These figures are intuitively sensible. Election outcomes can be decided
when large numbers of identifiers of one party vote for the other party.
This simple fact is highlighted when we look at the Republican-Democratic
party differential (i.e., the difference between the percentage of Democratic
party identifiers who voted for the Republican candidate *minus* the
percentage of Republican identifiers who voted for the Democratic
candidate). The differential *always* favored the Republicans, with the

TABLE 6.7   EFFECT OF ISSUES ON ELECTORAL BEHAVIOR, 1984

	1984 Vote	
Voting Pattern	Reagan	Mondale
Budget Deficit		
Republicans Voting for Reagan	3.6	
Republicans Voting for Mondale		- - -
Independents Voting for Reagan	5.1	
Independents Voting for Mondale		1.7
Democrats Voting for Reagan	.4	
Democrats Voting for Mondale		3.4
	9.1	5.1
Unemployment		
Republicans Voting for Reagan	1.9	
Republicans Voting for Mondale		- - -
Independents Voting for Reagan	1.7	
Independents Voting for Mondale		1.1
Democrats Voting for Reagan	.5	
Democrats Voting for Mondale		3.8
	4.2	4.9
War Fear		
Republicans Voting for Reagan	1.6	
Republicans Voting for Mondale		- - -
Independents Voting for Reagan	1.8	
Independents Voting for Mondale		1.2
Democrats Voting for Reagan	.3	
Democrats Voting for Mondale		3.4
	3.7	4.6

(Total N = 1,327)

smallest margin (3.5 percent) in 1976 and the largest in 1972 with a massive 15.4 percent.

Table 6.7 provides some insight as to factors producing behavior inconsistent with party identification. None of the three issues under consideration produced dramatic effects on the election outcome. Reagan's chief advantage was on the budget deficit, where overall he gained a net advantage of 4.0 percent when independents were included, but only a 0.6 percent advantage when they were omitted from the analysis. It was shown earlier that the inflation issue probably produced much of the motivation for Democratic partisan identifiers to vote for Reagan. In 1984, the shift of Democrats to Reagan on the single most important issue was much less pronounced but was clearly influential when independents are included. Further, it's clear that, given the patterns of independent support over the last two elections, Reagan substantially benefitted from their support in 1984.

TABLE 6.8   INFLUENCE OF ISSUES AND PARTY PREFERRED ON
ELECTORAL BEHAVIOR IN 1984

Voting Pattern	Reagan	Indifferent Reagan	Indifferent Mondale	Mondale
Budget Deficit				
Republican Voting for Reagan	4.6	26.8		
Republican Voting for Mondale			1.3	---
Independent Voting for Reagan	2.5	15.7		
Independent Voting for Mondale			7.1	.7
Democrat Voting for Reagan	.7	7.7		
Democrat Voting for Mondale			28.5	3.3
	7.8			4.0
Unemployment				
Republican Voting for Reagan	1.7	29.8		
Republican Voting for Mondale			1.4	---
Independent Voting for Reagan	.7	17.6		
Independent Voting for Mondale			7.5	---
Democrat Voting for Reagan	.3	7.8		
Democrat Voting for Mondale			28.2	3.8
	2.7			3.8
War Fear				
Republican Voting for Reagan	2.3	29.0		
Republican Voting for Mondale			1.4	---
Independent Voting for Reagan	---	17.3		
Independent Voting for Mondale			7.0	---
Democrat Voting for Reagan	.5	7.3		
Democrat Voting for Mondale			29.1	2.9
	2.8			2.9

(Total N = 1,327)

   Similar conclusions are drawn from Table 6.8 which shows patterns
of support very like those in the previous table. The budget deficit
produced a modest 3.8 percent net gain for Reagan, while the other
issues produced very modest net Democratic effects. Of these, unemployment had the largest effect (of slightly over 1.0 percent net Democratic
gain). Basically, the findings for 1984 were somewhat similar to those
obtained for the 1972 election in that no single issue dominated the
political landscape.

Summary
   As was noted at the outset of the previous section, an analysis of
the 1984 election outcome is hampered by the exclusion of the previous

vote variable from the CPS election study. This necessitated the construction of a surrogate measure of previous patterns of partisan support. For this purpose, party identification was used to show that in 1972 and in 1980 much of the shift in the electorate from one party to another from the prior election occurred largely among Democratic party identifiers. When, as a means of validation, I examined the 1980 election, it was found that the results were very similar to the standard aggregate-level analysis for 1980.

In the 1984 case, individual-level analyses previously had suggested that no single issue was especially influential at the individual level. Further, no single issue had the salience or unidirectional quality to have an effect, such as inflation had in 1980, in having a decisive effect on the election outcome. This was confirmed by the aggregate-level analysis for 1984, which showed that the budget deficit worked in Reagan's favor, although unemployment and concern over military involvement actually had a marginal pro-Democratic impact. What the aggregate-level analysis did suggest was that each of the elections examined in the 1972–84 period can be partially explained by partisan identifiers voting for the other party. This is also the case for 1984, although none of the issues examined fully explain the lopsided nature of Reagan's victory. There was no party mandate implied in Ronald Reagan's reelection victory. In order to understand the magnitude of the 1984 landslide, we must turn to other causes, such as the electorate's appraisal of the performance record of the administration over the previous four years.[28] President Reagan may have had an opportunity to mobilize the electorate on behalf of conservative policy goals. But, if so, he failed to take advantage of the possibility.

7

Making Sense of It All: Summary and Conclusions

The basic theme of this work is that issues can be important. They can be important in explaining both individual voting behavior and election outcomes. However, issues are not always important in explaining individual behavior or outcomes; and, issues important at the individual level do not necessarily explain aggregate phenomena.

Before issues can explain the latter, five conditions must be met. First, issues must be salient. If they are not important, then issues *ipso facto* have no influence. Second, issues must be linked in the voter's mind to a party. The voters must perceive one party as best able to handle a particular issue. Third, the issue must be salient to a significant percentage of the electorate. Many issues may arise in a campaign, but only a few have the potential for influencing the outcome. These issues are likely to be highly visible, perhaps emotional valence-type issues, with a high degree of symbolic content. Fourth, issues must work to the advantage of one party. An issue may be very salient, but if the electorate is divided between the parties with regard to the issue, or if voters are undecided between the parties, then the issue cannot have any significant influence on the election outcome. Fifth, issues must be able to explain behavior of the electorate over time, from one election to the next. Therefore, before an issue can affect individual behavior, it must possess the first two characteristics. But before it can explain the election outcome, all five qualities must be present. The individual-level analyses which have been performed for each of the elections over the 1972–1984 period serve as a conceptual link or bridge between individual actions and election outcomes.

Related to this primary concern with the relationship between issues and election outcomes are several themes that play a potentially significant role in understanding the relationship between actors and outcomes. Among them are questions relating to the kinds of decision rules voters use in making voting choices. Whether voters tend to vote retrospectively or, alternatively, include prospective components in their decision making relates directly to the question of whether voters utilize a simple reward-punishment or issue-priority approach to making electoral decisions. The approach adopted by voters, in turn, informs us as to the utility of the traditional valence-positional issue dichotomy and how parties and candidates may try to handle issues on which they may be vulnerable. This study of issues in presidential elections has also looked at the volatility of issue salience and the mutability of issue linkages to particular parties. These factors also influence the nature of campaign debate and party strategies.

In a larger sense, an understanding of the forces which shape election outcomes must take into account the role that mandates may play. Although this is a term used—and misused—by politicians, a policy mandate for a particular issue can exist only when it has been influential in determining the election outcome, and not merely because it was influential at the individual level. Moreover, to the extent a "mandate" exists, it may only be a signal from the voters to resolve a problem, and not a blueprint for specific policy action.

One work addressing the problem of an "absent mandate" suggests that any issue having a decisive effect on the outcome of an election is a valence-type issue. Indeed, politicians create, or attempt to create, valence-type issues for precisely this purpose. Although voters can agree upon the importance of an issue, and upon the conditions or problems that cause the issue to become salient, such an agreement offers little policy guidance. Paradoxically, emphasizing a problem voters regard as important does not necessarily mean that voters will agree that a particular party is best able to deal with it. To the extent that the electorate can quickly alter their partisan preferences on a particular issue, parties in power have little incentive to offer clear policy positions or to adhere to them even after they have been enunciated.[1]

Given these general observations, what happened in recent presidential elections? In the 1972 election, no single issue dominated the political agenda. None of the issues examined in that election (Vietnam, inflation, and crime) could account for the election outcome, although each issue worked marginally in favor of the Republicans at the aggregate level. The Vietnam issue is interesting for two reasons. First, although still the most salient issue in 1972, it had declined dramatically in importance from 1968. An issue which had the potential for damaging Republican chances had been at least partially defused by the gradual withdrawal of American forces. Second, the perceived extremism of the Democratic candidate may have served to reduce any opportunities for a Democratic advantage on this issue. Whereas Vietnam had the potential for turning into a valence issue, Mr. Nixon's handling of it, together with the Democratic candidate's shortcomings, actually allowed the Republicans to make a small marginal gain. Inflation and crime, seemingly valence issues that would work against Mr. Nixon, actually worked in his behalf, again suggesting that the effect of issues is dependent upon the campaign context and the perception of party competence in handling particular issues.

The 1976 election took place in an entirely different environment. Economic concerns predominated, especially unemployment and inflation. This election also illustrates the "reward-punishment" model of individual electoral behavior discussed earlier. Unemployment and inflation were both negatively associated with support for Mr. Ford, even though the issue-priority model predicts that voters concerned about inflation will prefer the Republican candidate because of the stress the Republican party traditionally has placed upon that issue, even if Republicans are the incumbents. The effects of unemployment and inflation are also characteristic of valence issues, serving to work against the incumbents. Although both unemployment and inflation were important at the individual level, only unemployment had a dramatic effect on the election outcome. Indeed, unemployment was the one issue that clearly decided the 1976 election in favor of Mr. Carter and the Democrats. Although the unemployment issue clearly decided the election, it did not provide a blueprint for action by the new administration, other than indicating that something had to be done about unemployment.

The 1980 election illustrates the volatility of issues, the mutability of issue-party ties and, as in 1976, the dramatic effects some issues can have upon elections. Inflation emerged as the single most important issue, followed by Iran, unemployment, and defense. Dramatic shifts favoring the Republicans occurred on the two economic issues. Unemployment worked only marginally in favor of the Democrats at the aggregate-level, in contrast to 1976 when it worked in a dramatic pro-Democratic direction. Inflation was the dominant issue and accounted for the election outcome. The other issues also produced net pro-Republican effects.

In contrast to 1976, the electorate responded in a manner consistent with an issue-priority effect. Although concern over inflation was positively related to support for the Republican candidate, Mr. Reagan, concern over unemployment was negatively related to Republican support (although the Democratic advantage was much reduced over 1976). More important for our purposes, while all issues can be shown to have been important at the individual level, inflation was the issue that decided the election outcome in favor of the Republicans. To the extent a mandate existed, it could be interpreted as a signal to do something about inflation; it is difficult to see how it could have been interpreted as a command for specific policy actions. However, the suggestion of an "issue-priority" effect might be taken to mean the electorate was willing to accept traditional Republican anti-inflation measures. Still, the apparent "flip-flopping" from reward-punishment to issue-priority voting over the 1976–80 period is troublesome. Indeed, the instability of party support on these valence-like issues is suggestive of a kind of "political debate" approach to understanding the relationship of partisan support to issues. Here, voting decisions are made based on the kinds of arguments put forth in the campaign and other short-term tactical considerations. Parties do not "own" issues; they merely borrow them. Consequently, the advantages that accrue to a party in one election may be highly ephemeral and add to the uncertainty of the tactical and strategic environment in which the parties and candidates are forced to operate and serves to discourage them from taking firm and consistent stands on issues. This, in turn, decreases the likelihood of elections serving as vehicles for the expression of the electorate's policy preferences.

The 1984 election appears in many respects to have been similar to that of 1972. No single issue predominated, as unemployment and inflation had in 1976 and 1980. The budget deficit, a newly emergent issue, along with concern over military involvement and unemployment, were the three most frequently cited concerns. As might be expected, no party benefitted dramatically from any single issue. Voters either were divided in support for the parties on an issue, or they were undecided or ambivalent as to which party could best deal with a particular issue. The budget deficit is fascinating because it lucidly illustrates how an apparent valence issue on which a party, in this case the Republicans, appears vulnerable can be neutralized through missteps by the opposition and clever appeals by the incumbents. Although it is clear that issues only occasionally have dramatic effects on election outcomes—albeit a mandate may be lacking—issues consistently produced strong individual-level effects when they were linked to party. To the extent that future research is aimed at exploring the importance of issue and policy voting, the relationship must be made explicit. Much of the analysis of issues has focused on the concept of valence.

The research presented here reinforces Alt's reservations about the valence-positional issue dichotomy.[2] An issue may have valence characteristics but still may not affect the outcome of an election. Rather than thinking of valence-positional dichotomies, it is probably more appropriate to think about issues and their effects in terms of a continuum. One area for future research, therefore, is to determine first when, and under what conditions, issues have effects consistent with valence (and reward-punishment) approaches to voting. It may be that, especially with economic issues, prospective issue-priority considerations consistent with positional issues operate only within certain ranges of performance.

When unemployment and/or inflation reach a certain level, reward-punishment takes over. At the same time, however, the evidence demonstrates conclusively that mediated prospective issue effects play a dominant role in individual voting behavior.

A related question to be asked is whether party system differences help explain issue effects. Do "pragmatic" or "weak" party systems (such as we have in the United States) produce effects different from "responsible" party systems such as in Canada or Britain? One would assume that in a system such as our own, in which the parties are relatively close ideologically, the likelihood of a particular issue having a dramatic effect on the election's outcome would increase. This is because the "costs" to a voter of voting for a party to which he or she has partisan attachment is less than in those highly polarized systems. Issues having reward-punishment effects should be more prevalent in these kinds of political systems, though findings suggest a greater likelihood, as well, for apparent "flip-flops" between past- and future-oriented voter responses to issues. This should be especially true of economic issues.

The focus here is on the dynamics of issues and their influence on election outcomes. I have not attempted to deal with the precise *determinants* of change. It is one thing to say that the context and salience of issues change over time, and something else to determine precisely what the mechanisms of change are. One plausible answer is that parties, in conjunction with party activists, act in rational utility-maximizing ways, constantly seeking means of enhancing their prospects for electoral success. As one issue begins to lose salience with the electorate, other issues may be brought to the fore. It may be wise to heed Riker's suggestion that:

> [W]e ignore the policies and platforms of the losers because these are the junk heap of history, the might-have-beens that never were. But we should not, I think, entirely overlook the losers and their goals for the losers provide the values of the future. The dynamics of politics is in the hands of the losers. It is they who decide when and how and whether to fight on. . . . Losers have nothing and can gain nothing unless they continue to try to bring about new political situations. This provides the motivation for change. . . . Losers are the ones who search out new strategies and stratagems and it is their use of heresthetics that provides the dynamics of politics.[3]

Riker shows how the parties of the National Republican-Whig-Republican tradition had been relatively unsuccessful throughout the first six decades of the nineteenth century, until they adopted the platform of commercial expansionism combined with the limitation of slavery.

By raising the salience of the slavery issue, the Republicans were able to split the Democrats, who struggled to contain the issue of slavery by arguing that it was of local concern.

More recently the Republican party has tried to increase its strength in the South by adopting positions on race that appeal to white southern Democrats. And, to an extent, they have succeeded. Carmines and Stimson, for instance, have shown that over the years the "macro-issue" of race has become increasingly salient, cutting across traditional partisan lines.[4] The budget deficit, an issue which has tended to be linked to the Republicans, was used by the Democrats in 1984 in an effort— albeit unsuccessful—to attract traditionally conservative voters who may have been fearful of a renewal of inflation and the high interest rates of the late 1970s.

The conscious efforts on the part of both parties to shift the issue agenda to more favorable grounds may have unfortunate consequences for the political system. Issue volatility, combined with uncertainty over the extent to which parties can "count" on certain issues working in their favor, may lead those who have been elected to offer contrived and poorly thought-out solutions to generally complex problems.[5] This, in turn, could act to erode faith in the ability of government to satisfactorily deal with problems. Indeed, rather than government simply being the victim of excessive demands placed upon it by voters, it may be, at least partially, to blame for the environment in which it is required to operate.[6] Given these conditions, it is not surprising that mandates may be difficult to obtain.

This discussion of issues also implies that we must be concerned with what have been termed "non-issues."[7] In understanding election outcomes, it can be as important to know which issues were not discussed as to know which issues were on the agenda. As I have noted previously, parties and candidates attempt to highlight certain issues. Unemployment and inflation have been cited as instances where Democrats and Republicans, respectively, stressed particular issues. The reverse, however, is the effort—sometimes successful, sometimes not—to suppress certain issues, or the fact that occasionally certain potential issues simply never attain visibility. Slavery seems to have been a kind of non-issue until the 1850s. It has been argued that race was an invisible issue during the 1930s and 1940s.[8] Watergate was a "non-issue" in 1972 despite efforts by Democrats to raise it to a higher level of visibility. It is simply not sufficient for issues to emerge because of purely objective "non-political" circumstances. Rather, problems and potential issues become issues only through the efforts by parties and politicians to gain tactical or strategic advantages.

Candidate policy proposals may be highly ambiguous because candidates seek to deflect damaging or potentially damaging issues. Thus, ambiguity may sometimes serve to "smother" a potential issue.[9] It can, in fact, be shown mathematically that clear policy stands, even when one is at the midpoint of public opinion, produce a less than optimal number of votes and can be defeated by strategies of ambiguity.[10] This, as well as the fact that parties can only make appeals on a limited number of issues without confusing the electorate and their core supporters, may explain why only a small number of issues seem to be dealt with in a given election.[11]

The suggested agenda can help redress the imbalance which I argue exists in studies of electoral behavior. More generally, I contend that previous research has been so concerned with the study of individual behavior that, until recently, more important questions concerning the *consequences* of individual-level phenomena have been all but ignored. This work has attempted to link the importance of individual-level issue concerns with the consequences of those concerns for election outcomes. But all of us, whether or not we are concerned with electoral behavior and elections, can benefit from efforts to comprehend more clearly the relationship between individual actions and their consequences for the societies in which we live.

8

Postscript:
The 1988 Presidential Election

In the aftermath of the November 8th election it may be useful to examine the general contours of the recent election campaign and to view how the general themes of this book relate to recent events. As with previous elections, a brief review of the dynamics and key events in the campaign is in order.

The 1988 election was the first in twenty years, since 1968, when an incumbent (excluding Gerald Ford) was not running for reelection. The uncertainty surrounding the ultimate outcome was consequently greater than any other election in this period. As the 1988 political season dawned, no candidate in either party appeared as an outstanding favorite.

Although George Bush entered 1988 as the generally acknowledged frontrunner within the Republican party, he certainly wasn't seen as having a "lock" on the nomination. Bush faced an apparently strong challenger in Sen. Robert Dole, as well as opposition from Rep. Jack Kemp, fundamentalist leader Pat Robertson, and other lesser candidates.[1] Bush also tended to be regarded as a candidate whose support, though quite broad within the party, was not strongly committed. A common view was that any early Bush setbacks would lead to a mass exodus from Bush to one of the other candidates. Bush's establishment credentials, it was believed, might not play well in a Republican party increasingly dominated by populist conservatives.[2] In particular, any past association with what was viewed as the Rockefeller liberal wing of the party could be deadly, even given Bush's assertion that he was now a "Reaganite." Additionally, Bush hadn't been helped by the Iran-Contra scandal, with the continuing questions and innuendo concerning the roles of President Reagan and himself. This, it was felt, could provide ammunition for Republican challengers as well as for the Democrats in the fall campaign.

Further, although Bush might have benefitted from President Reagan's popularity, it had fallen precipitately following the Iran-Contra revelations in November 1986 and the continuing media coverage throughout the winter. Prior to the scandal, Reagan's popularity had reached nearly 70 percent in the summer of 1986, but it had dropped quickly to around 40 percent by early 1987; until near the very end of his presidency, Reagan didn't regain his earlier support.[3] Even in April and May of 1988, the administration had been shaken by claims that Mrs. Reagan had frequently consulted astrologers and had used their prognostications to influence her husband's decisions.

Given this environment, conditions weren't the best for George Bush's political future, but as we will see later, certain other political and economic factors were clearly not all unfavorable. Still, Bush in early 1988 gave one the impression of a beleaguered politician, and this perception was reinforced by his stunning defeat in the Iowa caucus.[4] Although he had not been expected to defeat Sen. Robert Dole, who was virtually a favorite son in that farmbelt state, Bush's ignominious third-place finish cast grave doubts on his viability as a Presidential contender.

As the Republican presidential candidates moved into New Hampshire, it seemed possible that Dole's momentum coming out of Iowa could carry him to victory in New Hampshire. This would have put him in a very strong position to win the nomination, in spite of the Bush campaign's presumed strength in the southern states that were holding primaries on "Super Tuesday." After the election results in New Hampshire on February 15 were known, however, it was obvious that Dole's presidential hopes had suffered a devastating setback.[5] Favored in the primary's final hours to defeat Vice-President Bush, Dole was stunned by his opponent's come-from-behind victory, which many attributed to tough commercials aired by the Bush campaign suggesting the likelihood of Dole's supporting a move to raise taxes if elected.[6]

George Bush's victory made him the odds-on favorite for the nomination, and with his enormous victories over his opponents in the "Super Tuesday" primaries, the race was effectively over.[7] Bush sailed through the other primaries, and opponents, including Senator Dole, soon abandoned any hope of stopping the Vice-President.

The road to the Democratic nomination was somewhat more difficult for Governor Michael Dukakis. As the 1988 presidential season opened, there seemed relatively little to distinguish Dukakis from his opponents, who included former Arizona governor Bruce Babbitt, Rep. Richard Gephardt of Missouri, Sen. Al Gore of Tennessee, the Rev. Jesse Jackson, Sen. Paul Simon of Illinois, and Gary Hart, who had reentered the race the previous May following accusations of sexual improprieties.[8]

Although Richard Gephardt won the Iowa primary and established himself as the nominal frontrunner, Dukakis's third-place finish managed to improve on earlier expectations for the northeastern, ethnic governor. It also left him well positioned for the New Hampshire primary the following week. As a next-door neighbor, Dukakis had a distinct advantage over the rest of the field. And a clear Dukakis victory, with Gephardt finishing a poor second and Simon a distant third, placed Dukakis in a fairly strong position relative to the other candidates.[9] Still, the upcoming southern primaries on "Super Tuesday" should not have boded well for Dukakis, given the presence of the generally acknowledged "southern candidate," Al Gore, and more especially Jesse Jackson, who was thought to have an excellent chance of mobilizing a monolithic black vote in support of his candidacy. Additionally, Gephardt posed a potential threat to Dukakis in the South, given Gephardt's populist rhetoric on trade and economic policy and related efforts to portray himself as a moderate. In fact, although both Gore and Jackson scored substantial wins on Super Tuesday, Dukakis was able to carry Florida and Texas and managed to pick up a substantial number of delegates in other states through clever targeting of districts.

Perhaps more important than the delegate totals, the "Super Tuesday" primaries fundamentally altered the structure of candidate competition by crippling Richard Gephardt's candidacy, forcing him to exit the race soon thereafter. This left only Dukakis, Jackson, and Gore as the three viable candidates in the race.[10] By positioning himself as a centrist relative to Jackson and Gore, Dukakis managed to solidify his position. Although the Massachusetts governor suffered embarrassing setbacks in Illinois and Michigan, he ran off a series of important primary victories beginning with Wisconsin and New York. The New York primary ended Gore's chances of victory, thus making it a two-person race. Given Jackson's high "negatives" and perceived left-wing stance, and aided by the inevitable resources that flow to the frontrunner, Dukakis coasted through May and June, wrapping up the nomination in seemingly effortless fashion.[11]

In the very early days of the presidential campaign, George Bush had held a very comfortable lead over Michael Dukakis in most of the surveys. A *Los Angeles Times* survey in mid-December of 1987 had shown Bush with a 49 to 23 percent lead over his future opponent. By March and April of the election year, however, the lead had tightened considerably. A Gallup/*Newsweek* survey taken at the end of March gave Bush a narrow 49 to 44 percent lead, and by late April Bush's lead had been cut to a razor-thin and statistically insignificant 45 to 43 point edge. Soon thereafter the Bush campaign seemed to go into an irreversible slide. By mid-May virtually all polling organizations were reporting a substantial lead for Dukakis. Gallup showed Bush trailing by 16 points (54 to 38) in mid-May, and an ABC–*Washington Post* survey placed Dukakis's lead at 53 to 40 percent during the last week of May.[12]

Dukakis maintained his lead through June and July, though there was some evidence of a tightening of the race. Even so, Dukakis came roaring out of the Democratic convention with what most polls suggested was a 17–18 point lead.[13] This occurred in spite of the controversy surrounding the Bentsen vice-presidential nomination and the related snub (or perceived snub) of Jesse Jackson. Indeed, the tension in the week just prior to the convention may have provided a net plus for Dukakis.

By the time of the Republican convention in mid-August there was evidence that Bush, though still trailing Dukakis, had rebounded to some extent. The flap over Dukakis's alleged mental health problems and questions concerning whether he had sought psychiatric treatment helped to tarnish his image. Other factors may also have helped account for Bush's partial rebound: The post-convention Dukakis "bounce" had begun to fade and was being replaced by a perception of Jackson as the dominant force at the Atlanta lovefest, a view that could serve to alienate white conservatives. Also, Bush's "values" attack against Dukakis, which will be explored later, was arguably beginning to exact a toll. Still, it appeared that Bush's chances for keeping the White House in Republican hands were not wholly favorable.

There is no need to recount in detail all the events of the post-Republican convention period. As we know, George Bush got a tremendous, much-needed surge of support following the convention—in spite of the furor over his selection of Sen. Dan Quayle of Indiana for Vice-President and the resulting controversy over Quayle's National Guard service. One survey gave Bush a 9-point lead just after the convention, and although there was some apparent slippage, Bush never, according to the public polls, relinquished his lead.[14] The only apparent effect of the televised debates was to strengthen Bush's then-current support. And although there was a flurry of speculation toward the very end of the campaign that Dukakis was closing the gap, he simply proved unable to stop the Bush bandwagon.[15] The polling trends in the Bush-Dukakis race are shown in Figure 8.1.

The 1988 election proved to be yet another major disappointment for the presidential aspirations of the Democratic party and raised the specter of a Republican party almost totally dominant at the presidential level. Bush's ability to hold onto the South—the strongest region for the Vice-President—and his retention of core Republican identifiers in the rest of the country proved more than sufficient for victory.[16] George Bush had seemingly snatched victory from the jaws of defeat.

Certainly one of the intriguing questions in this and other elections is whether the outcome resulted primarily from the short-term dynamics of the election or, alternatively, from longer-term political factors. Among the potential short-term factors, one would certainly include the elec-

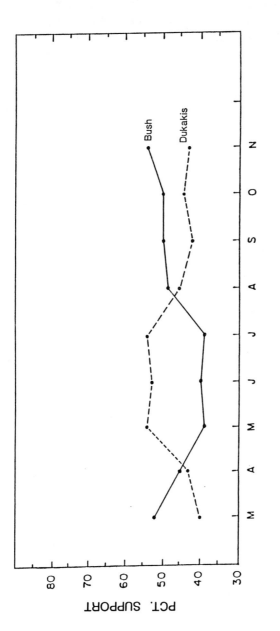

Figure 8.1.   Bush–Dukakis Race, March to November, 1988

torate's assessments of the candidates, the issues raised and the most salient issues of the campaign, the skill (or lack of skill) in manipulating those issues, the decisiveness of the primary battles. Martin Wattenberg has suggested at least one interpretation of the 1988 election that emphasizes the importance of short-term forces. Wattenberg suggests that Governor Dukakis's long struggle with Jesse Jackson for the Democratic nomination—while temporarily helpful by focusing media attention on Dukakis—exaggerated his true strength in the electorate. Wattenberg argues that a key to understanding the 1988 election outcome was to a great extent determined by the long, divisive struggle Dukakis had to endure for the nomination.[17]

Another view expressed during the campaign was that Bush's success stemmed from a long-term shift in key-group support—from the Democratic to Republican presidential candidates.[18] But my own view is that short-term forces, namely issue concerns, explain election outcomes—at least in certain circumstances.[19]

I have so far avoided explicit mention of issues. What role did they play in the most recent presidential election and its outcome? Although I'm precluded from conducting a systematic analysis due to lack of available data, a brief examination of issues and their potential effects on the 1988 presidential campaign is in order.

Presidential elections, of course, are always to a great extent concerned with character and leadership qualities. The 1988 contest was no exception: Among the characteristics evaluated were Bush's difficulties in the pre-convention period with the "wimp" image and Dukakis's bland, unemotional, technocratic style and demeanor.[20] The focus in this book, however, has been on issues. Questions relating to character and images of the candidates or parties may be influential and can work for or against candidate or officeholder, but governing is ultimately about policy and issues.

The 1988 campaign highlights the retrospective-prospective dimension that I've addressed in earlier chapters. George Bush and the Republicans probably viewed themselves as benefitting, for the most part, from the accomplishments of the Reagan administration. Dukakis and the Democrats stood to gain if they could fight the election in terms of the future.

Dukakis essentially needed to negate, or at least reduce, the valence-issue themes of "peace and prosperity" by pointing to the thunderclouds over the horizon. He, in effect, had the task of convincing voters to ignore recent outcomes (low inflation and unemployment, for instance) and focus on past policy and the future consequences of those policies. Dukakis might well have benefitted to the extent he could convince voters to examine their electoral choices in Downsian terms.[21] This is not to say that Bush ignored the prospective element; indeed, I would argue that Bush was able to substantially reduce his disadvantages on the prospective dimension through his ability to frame the campaign agenda. Nor was Dukakis devoid of issues that would allow him to reduce the Republican advantages by fighting the election as a referendum on the Reagan years. Still, each candidate had distinctive strengths going into the campaign, which reflected their respective strengths along the temporal dimension.

In many respects, of course, the 1988 election was indeed a referendum on the Reagan administration. And to a substantial extent, that administration had a record of solid accomplishments. By mid-1988 inflation was much lower than in the last year of the Carter administration, and while it had risen slightly since 1987, it was still not seen as reaching danger levels. Unemployment had declined steadily since late 1982, during the throes of the recession, and had fallen to under 6 percent in 1988. The United States was in the sixth year of an economic expansion. Interest levels remained relatively low.[22]

In the area of foreign policy the United States and Soviet Union appeared to be moving toward a new détente. The internal changes within the Soviet Union being brought about by Mikhail Gorbachev's new policies of *glasnost* (openness) and *perestroika* (restructuring) held forth the promise that the Soviets would be preoccupied with domestic reforms for the foreseeable future and were likely to offer a significantly reduced threat to the United States and the West. Reagan and Gorbachev had held three full-scale summit meetings, and there appeared a palpable reduction of tensions between the two countries. A treaty banning an entire class of nuclear weapons in Europe had been signed in December 1987, and there were hopes not only for a strategic arms agreement that would reduce long-range nuclear forces by as much as 50 percent, but also a conventional arms reduction treaty that would significantly reduce NATO and Warsaw pact forces in Europe.

The judicious application of U.S. force in the Reagan years had also had a positive effect. Steady U.S. support for the Afghan guerrillas fighting the Soviet-backed Kabul regime had led to the announcement of a Soviet withdrawal from Afghanistan. U.S. support for Jonas Savimbi's UNITA guerrilla force in Angola had produced negotiations between Cuba, South Africa, and the Marxist Angolan government to remove Cuban and South African forces from Angola, which could in turn allow for a settlement of the Namibian problem. Further, U.S. diplomacy had helped in removing President Ferdinand Marcos of the Philippines from power, leading to a democratic transition in that nation. The regime of "Baby Doc" Duvalier in Haiti had been ousted, with at least tacit U.S. approval.

Exit polls taken on election day revealed that voters were almost evenly divided in their assessment of the Reagan administration. Fifty percent of voters indicated that the nation should "continue in the same direction," while the same percentage believed the nation needed "a new direction."[23] Thus, neither Bush nor Dukakis appeared to achieve a decisive edge by framing the campaign debate as a referendum on the Reagan administration. But other issues or potential issues existed, which suggested that the Republicans could be quite vulnerable. The economy seemed to be a double-edged sword. While outward signs were favorable—low inflation and unemployment, relatively low interest rates—two other economic issues constituted potential time-bombs for Bush and the Republicans: The budget deficit, which had grown tremendously under Reagan, was seen as a major threat for the future prosperity of the nation and was cited in post-election surveys as the most important problem facing the nation; relatedly, the growing trade deficit between the United States and its trading partners also constituted what many viewed as a threat to U.S. jobs and industry.

These two issues held no inconsiderable potential for the Democrats. Still, both issues—unlike inflation, unemployment, or higher interest rates—are of the type that are difficult to link (in the voter's mind) to their individual circumstances. They are also issues that voters may have difficulty linking, either positively or negatively, to one party or the other, either because of a belief that neither party can handle the problem or because the issues are so complex that clear differences between the parties aren't distinguished. Further, the budget deficit, seemingly a valence issue, could be neutralized in part by criticizing the use of higher taxes to finance the deficit. This, indeed, was what Bush appeared to do, and quite successfully. In fact, the budget deficit never became the source of contention one might have thought. Dukakis decried the deficit, but his own plan to deal with it, which he claimed wouldn't include tax increases, may not have seemed credible and left room for Bush's counterattack, i.e., that Dukakis would, in fact, raise taxes once in office. Relatedly, elevation of the issue also left Dukakis vulnerable on the budgetary problems of Massachusetts. The budget deficit, consequently, may have been a nonstarter for Dukakis. Indeed, there is considerable evidence that Bush's hardline stance against tax increases played a considerable role in his victory. One study showed that among voters who liked the candidates' stances on taxes, Bush held a 6-point advantage.[24] Likewise, while the trade deficit held potential for Dukakis, Bush was in a position to accuse Dukakis of adopting a protectionist strategy to solve the problem. That Bush tactic, again, may have served to partially neutralize the issue. By transferring the terms of debate on some of these questions from "ends" to "means," Bush was positioned to reduce the potency of some of his opponent's heaviest attacks. Indeed, surveys indicated that among voters citing all economic problems— including the budget deficit—as important to their vote, they divided evenly. Further, voters split about evenly on the future of the economy. Bush gained a substantial advantage among the 50 percent not worried about future economic conditions but also managed to win 30 percent of those who did worry about the future.[25]

Bush might have been more vulnerable on foreign policy. The Iran-Contra affair and the U.S. failure to remove General Manuel Noriega in Panama might have been the Achilles heel of the Bush campaign. Both, but certainly the former, were not as amenable to the kinds of strategies that were adopted as were the economic issues. Both were clearly valence issues, the nature of which prevented Bush from attempting to convert to positional issues to reduce the damage. Further, the Noriega problem tied in with the problem of drug abuse, which gained momentum in 1987 and 1988 as a critical problem area. Neither issue, however, seemed to achieve a great deal of prominence in the campaign and seemingly failed to provide significant leverage for Dukakis; among those citing international affairs as important to their vote decision, Bush won decisively.[26] Another issue, AIDS, was treated with kid gloves by both candidates. Bush and Dukakis steered away from any serious discussion of AIDS, and the disease never emerged as a visible issue in the campaign.

One issue that appeared to attain enormous resonance in the campaign can be clustered under the general heading of "values." Virtually no observer prior to the 1988 political season would have suggested that crime and the Pledge of Allegiance would constitute major issues during the campaign. But that is what happened. By tagging Dukakis as hostile to traditional values by virtue of his veto of a bill passed by the Massachusetts legislature mandating that public school teachers lead their students in the Pledge of Allegiance, Bush was enormously successful in portraying Dukakis as hostile toward "traditional" American values. While Dukakis might have partially nullified the effectiveness of this attack by claiming that his actions upheld traditional notions of religious liberty, he failed to do so and was consequently politically wounded. Likewise, the Willie Horton advertisement, concerning the furloughed convict who had terrorized a Maryland couple, served brilliantly to portray Dukakis as "soft on crime." While only 12 and 10 percent, respectively, thought the pledge issue or the furlough program were important issues, Bush won overwhelmingly among this group. On the related issue of the death penalty, Bush was overwhelmingly (75 to 25 percent) favored among those who advocated the death penalty.[27]

Dukakis never seemed to recover from the values attacks, which were a focal point of the campaign. Once Dukakis had been painted with the "liberal" label on these as well as other issues, the campaign was, in my view, lost. And indeed, the "L" word provided a convenient political shorthand for Dukakis and struck at the heart of Dukakis's claims to be "tough on crime." Both issues served to highlight, to the Republicans' advantage, the social liberalism of the national Democratic party, in contrast to the Republican party. At the same time, the Republicans were discriminating in their use of particular issues; for example, the party supported a ban on abortion, but abortion was rarely, if ever, a centerpiece of the campaign. Still, Bush held a clear advantage among the nearly one-third of survey respondents who said it was an important issue.[28]

These tentative analyses suggest that, unlike 1976 and 1980, no single issue had the kind of dramatic effect on the outcome as unemployment and inflation had in those years. Nonetheless, there is evidence that the social issues just noted, along with Bush's no-tax stance, may have been more than sufficient to guarantee a third consecutive Republican presidential victory. There was no inevitability, however, in this outcome. Rather, one would have to concede that the Vice-President did a brilliant job of controlling the issue agenda in a way that set the stage for his election.

This election gives us a classic example of how candidates and parties, by defining the terms of debate and the issue agenda, can seize the initiative, and, to a substantial degree, control their own destiny. Bush managed to frame the campaign debate in a way that reduced his own vulnerabilities on issues like the deficit and to those generally concerned about the economic future. Simultaneously, he managed to introduce a dimension in the form of the values attack, which allowed him to seize and control the political agenda for the duration of the campaign. But Bush's strategy for victory still leaves open the question of mandates. Given the way mandates have been defined in this study, it may well be that George Bush has taken into the White House a mandate on the tax issue and the aforementioned social issues. Still, even if the kinds of issues that appeared so effective in the campaigns were decisive for the election outcome, it may help very little in allowing the new president to deal effectively with the pressing economic problems, especially the deficit, that this country continues to face.[29] This is not the fault of politicians. Rather, it simply reflects the structure and dynamics of presidential campaigns. The actions that candidates are required to take in order to win an election may inhibit their ability to govern once the mantle of leadership falls on their shoulders.

Appendix A: Construction
of Analysis Variables

Variables constructed for the individual-level analyses are as follows:

Individual Voting Models

Vote: Vote is a dichotomous dependent variable, coded 1 for Republican Voter, 0 for Democratic Voter. Those voting for minor party candidates, for Independent candidate John Anderson in 1980, and those respondents refusing to indicate for whom they voted were excluded from the analysis. This variable is identical for each election.

Republican Party ID: Two dichotomous dummy variables are included in the analysis to represent Republican and Democratic party identifiers. This variable is constructed from the traditional seven-point party identification scale. Strong and weak Republican identifiers are coded 1; all others, including Independent Republicans, Independents, and Democrats, are coded 0.

Democratic Party ID: This variable is coded in the same manner as described above. Strong and weak Democratic identifiers are coded as 1; all others are coded 0.

Issue and Issue-Party Variables

1972

Issues: The three most frequently cited problems are Vietnam, Inflation, and Crime. Voters citing Vietnam, Inflation, or Crime as the single most important problem facing the country are coded 1; all others are coded 0. Crime also includes categories for "moral decay" and drug use.

Issue-Party Variables: All voters citing the Republicans as the party best able to deal with the single most important problem facing the country (Vietnam, Inflation, Crime) are coded 1. Those citing the Democrats as most competent are coded −1; those undecided or indifferent, 0.

1976

Issues: The four most frequently cited problems are Unemployment, Inflation, Economy (General Economic Problems), and Crime. All voters citing one of these as the single most important problem facing the country are coded 1, otherwise 0.

Issue-Party Variables: All voters citing the Republicans as the party best able to deal with the single most important problem facing the country are coded 1. Those citing the Democrats as most competent are coded −1; those undecided or indifferent, 0.

1980

Issues: The four most frequently cited problems are Inflation, Iran, Unemployment, and Defense (military preparedness). All voters citing one of these as the single most important problem facing the country are coded 1, otherwise 0.

Issue-Party Variables: All voters citing the Republicans as the party best able to deal with the single most important problem are coded 1. Those citing Democrats as most competent, −1; those undecided or indifferent, 0.

1984

Issues: The three most frequently cited problems are Budget Deficit, "War Fear" (representing combined responses for those concerned about conventional and nuclear conflict), and Unemployment. All voters citing one of these problems as "most important" are coded 1; otherwise 0.

Issue-Party Variables: All voters citing the Republicans as the party best able to deal with the single most important problem cited are coded 1; those citing Democrats, −1; those undecided or indifferent, 0.

Appendix B:
Statistical Techniques

Until recent years, the most used and most commonly accepted multivariate statistical technique was Ordinary Least Squares (OLS) regression. This technique is perfectly acceptable if we assume an interval level, or continuous, dependent variable. However, social scientists are handicapped by the fact that very few of the variables they work with are truly continuous. OLS can cause special problems when the dependent variables are simple dichotomies such as whether one votes Democratic or Republican, as is the case with this study. OLS is also a risky procedure for trichotomous cases, such as when individuals may rate presidential performance, or economic performance, of the government in terms of good, fair, or poor. For polytomous cases, the most obvious example is the traditional seven-point party identification measure.

The problem with all of these cases, but especially with the dichotomous situation, is the assumption of constant covariance of the error term. In predicting vote, the only observed values are 1 (voting Republican) and 0 (voting Democratic). This immediately violates the assumption of constant variance.

Moreover, since OLS assumes a linear relationship between the dependent and independent variables, predicted values in the dichotomous case can be either greater than, or less than, one, which is a logical impossibility.[1] Probit avoids the weaknesses of OLS regression by assuming a nonlinear relationship between the dependent and independent variables. This relationship, in fact, represents the "normal curve." In general, the observed behavior (the explanatory variables) is assumed to follow some specific probability distribution function.

Many social scientists are beginning to adopt techniques widely used by econometricians. Probit and logit are two of the most widely accepted techniques. Although probit was used in this study, either technique is suitable for the dichotomous case. In this particular case, the former was selected due to the availability (and non-availability) of software packages. The analysis of data utilizing probit (as well as logit) techniques relies upon maximum likelihood estimates. This involves solving for a system of nonlinear equations. For this study, the McKelvey-Zavoina N-probit program was used.[2]

Unfortunately, probit coefficients cannot be interpreted in the same manner as OLS coefficients. As Fiorina has noted, a probit coefficient does not tell us anything directly about the probability of the occurrence of the dependent variable which is being explained. Before we can make any assertion concerning the impact of an independent variable, X_i, it is necessary to know the *values* at which the other independent variables are being held constant.

The crucial question in probit analysis is where the individual is placed on the probability curve. If he is at either of the tails of the distribution, represented by either a very high or very low probability of voting for the Republican candidate, a unit change in X_i will produce a much smaller effect than for an individual who lies much closer to the middle or the "fat" part of the curve.[3]

Probit, then, does offer a way around some of the somewhat naive assumptions implicit in the more familiar regression techniques. But the chief cautionary note which is in order is that interpretation is not quite so straightforward as more traditional approaches.

Notes

Chapter 1

1. One very recent study by Gregory Markus explicitly examines both individual-level and aggregate issue effects. See Gregory B. Markus, "The Impact of Personal and National Economic Conditions on the Presidential Vote: A Pooled Cross Section Analysis," *American Journal of Political Science*, 32 (1988), pp. 137–154.

2. The idea of classifying issues was first proposed by Donald Stokes, "Spatial Models of Party Competition," *American Political Science Review*, 57 (1963), p. 373. Also see David Butler and Donald Stokes, *Political Change in Britain* (New York: St. Martin's Press, 1969), p. 390.

Chapter 2

1. Steven Rosenstone, *Forecasting Presidential Elections* (New Haven and London: Yale University Press, 1983), ch. 1.

2. Angus Campbell, Gerald Gurin, and Warren E. Miller, *The Voter Decides* (Evanston, Illinois: Row, Peterson, 1984).

3. Angus Campbell, Philip E. Converse, Warren E. Miller, and Donald E. Stokes, *The American Voter* (New York: John Wiley and Sons, 1960).

4. Angus Campbell, et al., *The American Voter*, pp. 172–179. For a more lengthy analysis of *The American Voter* findings, see Herbert Asher, *Presidential Elections and American Politics* (Homewood, Ill.: Dorsey Press, 1988), pp. 94–97.

5. Philip Converse, "The Nature of Belief Systems in Mass Publics," in David Apter, ed., *Ideology and Discontent* (New York: Free Press, 1964), pp. 206–261.

6. Philip Converse, "Attitudes and Non-Attitudes: The Continuation of a Dialogue," in Edward Tufte, ed., *The Quantitative Analysis of Social Problems* (Reading, Mass.: Addison-Wesley, 1976), pp. 168–178.

7. This is a basic assumption in the spatial theory of voting. As pointed out by Enelow and Hinich, there is a distinct absence of incentives for voters to acquire much information about candidates; also, candidates may have reason to be vague and ambiguous. They argue that in mass elections predictive labels such as party or ideology are used as a kind of shorthand in making decisions concerning issue positions. The theory of spatial voting is not dealt with here, constituting, as it does, a radically different approach to electoral behavior. That is not to say that spatial theory isn't an important contribution to the voting

literature. I happen to believe it represents an important new approach to understanding electoral motivations. I also draw on elements of spatial theory in discussing candidate and campaign strategies. For an excellent introduction to spatial voting, see James M. Enelow and Melvin J. Hinich, *The Spatial Theory of Voting* (Cambridge: Cambridge University Press, 1984).

8. Samuel A. Kirkpatrick, William Lyons, and Michael Fitzgerald, "Candidates, Parties, and Issues in the American Electorate," *American Politics Quarterly*, 3 (1975), pp. 247–285.

9. Gregory B. Markus and Philip E. Converse, "A Dynamic Simultaneous Equation Model of Electoral Choice," *American Political Science Review*, 73 (1979), pp. 1055–1070.

10. Donald R. Kinder and Robert P. Abelson, "Appraising Presidential Candidates: Personality and Affect in the 1980 Campaign," paper presented at the Annual Meeting of the American Political Science Association, New York City, September 3–6, 1981.

11. Arthur H. Miller and Martin Wattenberg, "Throwing the Rascals Out: Policy and Performance Evaluations of Presidential Candidates, 1952–1980," *American Political Science Review*, 79 (1985), pp. 359–372.

12. See Paul R. Abramson, John H. Aldrich, and David W. Rohde, *Change and Continuity in the 1984 Elections* (Washington, D.C.: CQ Press, 1986), p. 191.

13. Morris Fiorina, *Retrospective Voting in American National Elections* (New Haven and London: Yale University Press, 1981), p. 185.

14. V. O. Key, Jr., *The Responsible Electorate: Rationality in Presidential Voting, 1936–1960* (Cambridge, Mass.: Harvard University Press, 1966).

15. Anthony Downs, *An Economic Theory of Democracy* (New York: Harper and Row, 1957).

16. See Fiorina, esp. chs. 8, 9, and 10.

17. Miller and Wattenberg, pp. 359–372.

18. James H. Kuklinski and Darrel M. West, "Economic Expectations and Voting Behavior in the United States House and Senate Elections," *American Political Science Review*, 73 (1979), pp. 1055–1070.

19. Hugh L. LeBlanc and Mary Beth Merrin, "Parties, Issues and Candidates: Another Look at Responsible Parties," *Western Political Quarterly*, 31 (1978), pp. 523–534; also see David Repass, "Issue Salience and Party Choice," *American Political Science Review*, 60 (1971), pp. 389–400.

20. Norman H. Nie, Sidney Verba, and John R. Petrocik, *The Changing American Voter* (Cambridge, Mass.: Harvard University Press, 1979).

21. See esp. Benjamin I. Page, *Choices and Echoes in Presidential Elections* (Chicago: Univ. of Chicago Press, 1978), ch. 6.

22. Key, *The Responsible Electorate*.

23. Harold D. Clarke, Marianne C. Stewart and Gary Zuk, "Politics, Economics and Party Popularity in Britain, 1979–83," *Electoral Studies*, 5 (1986), pp. 123–141. Also see D. Roderick Kiewiet, *Macroeconomics and Micropolitics* (Chicago: University of Chicago Press, 1983). Kiewiet uses the term policy-oriented voting to describe the phenomenon I describe as issue-priority voting.

24. Douglas A. Hibbs, Jr., "Political Parties and Macroeconomic Policy," *American Political Science Review*, 76 (1977), pp. 83–93; also see Douglas A. Hibbs, Jr., *The American Political Economy* (Cambridge: Harvard University Press).

25. Clarke, et al., "Politics, Economics and Party Popularity in Britain, 1979–83."

26. Edward G. Carmines and James A. Stimson, "The Two Faces of Issue Voting," *American Political Science Review*, 74 (1986), pp. 78–91.

27. Butler and Stokes, pp. 177–178.

28. Also see Fiorina, *Retrospective Voting in American National Elections*, pp. 18–19. Fiorina also addresses the question, as I do, that, assuming a clear valence-positional dichotomy, valence and positional issues might correlate with retrospective versus prospective voting.

29. James E. Alt, *The Politics of Economic Decline* (Cambridge: Cambridge University Press, 1979).

30. Donald R. Kinder and D. Roderick Kiewiet, "Economic Discontent and Political Behavior: The Role of Personal Grievances and Collective Economic Judgments in Congressional Voting," *American Journal of Political Science*, 23 (1979), pp. 495–527. Also see Kiewiet, *Macroeconomics and Micropolitics*.

31. As Kinder and Kiewiet note, this does not gainsay the possibility that voters may "selfishly" believe national economic performance is directly related to their own financial well being. It should also be noted that there is a debate over whether cross-sectional or aggregate-level data are best for examining the question of individual vs. sociotropic voting. Gerald Kramer, in an influential article, argues that survey level data alternate "pocketbook" effects, and that aggregate analyses support the "pocketbook" hypotheses. See Gerald Kramer, "The Ecological Fallacy Revisited: Aggregate Versus Individual-Level Findings in Elections, and Sociotropic Voting," *American Political Science Review*, 77 (1983), pp. 92–111.

32. M. Stephen Weatherford, "Economic Voting and the 'Symbolic Politics' Argument: A Reinterpretation and Synthesis," *American Political Science Review*, 77 (1983), pp. 158–174.

33. Patricia Johnston Conover, "The Influence of Group Identifications on Political Perception and Evaluation," *Journal of Politics*, 46 (1984), pp. 760–785.

34. Gerald Kramer, "Short Term Fluctuations in U.S. Voting Behavior, 1896–1964," *American Political Science Review*, 65 (1971), pp. 131–143.

35. George J. Stigler, "General Economic Conditions and National Elections," *American Economic Review*, 63 (1973), pp. 160–167.

36. Francisco Arcelus and Allan H. Meltzer, "The Effect of Aggregate Economic Variables on Congressional Election," *American Political Science Review*, 69 (1975), pp. 1232–1239.

37. Edward R. Tufte, "Determinants of the Outcomes of Midterm Congressional Elections," *American Political Science Review*, 69 (1975), pp. 812–826.

38. Howard S. Bloom and Douglas H. Price, "Voter Response to Short-Run Economic Conditions: The Asymmetric Effects of Prosperity and Recession," *American Political Science Review*, 19 (1975), pp. 1240–1254.

126   *Notes*

39. Rosenstone, *Forecasting Presidential Elections.* Also see Ray C. Fair, "The Effect of Economic Events on Votes for President," *The Review of Economics and Statistics,* 60 (1978), pp. 159–173.

40. See, for instance, Henry Chappell, "Presidential Popularity and Macro-economic Performance: Are Voters Really So Naive," *Review of Economics and Statistics,* 65 (1983), pp. 385–392. Also, Henry Chappell and William R. Keech, "A New View of Political Accountability for Economic Performance," *American Political Science Review,* 79 (1985), pp. 10–27. An especially interesting work is Kristen R. Monroe and Maurice Levy, "Economic Expectations, Economic Uncertainty, and Presidential Popularity," in Kristen R. Monroe, ed., *The Political Process and Economic Change* (New York: Agathon Press, 1983), pp. 214–232.

41. Key, *The Responsible Electorate.*

42. Michael S. Lewis-Beck, "Comparative Economic Voting: Britain, France, Germany, Italy," *American Journal of Political Science,* 30 (1986), pp. 315–346.

43. Michael S. Lewis-Beck, "Economics and the American Voter: Past, Present and Future," *Political Behavior,* 10 (1988), pp. 5–21.

44. Fiorina, *Retrospective Voting in American National Elections.*

45. Kiewiet, *Macroeconomics and Micropolitics.*

46. Miller and Wattenberg, pp. 359–372.

47. For two examples of work supporting these assertions, see Donald R. Kinder and Walter Mebane, Jr., "Politics and Economics in Everyday Life," in Kristen Monroe, ed., *The Political Process and Economic Change;* also see Euel Elliott and Rose Godfrey, "Public Evaluations of Economic Performance: The United States, 1976–84," in Harold D. Clarke, Marianne C. Stewart and Gary Zuk, eds., *Politics, Policy and the Economy: Canada, Great Britain, and the United States* (Pittsburgh: Pittsburgh University Press, 1989).

48. Donald E. Stokes, "Some Dynamic Elements of Contests for the Presidency," *American Political Science Review,* 60 (1960), pp. 19–28.

49. See Gerald Kramer, "Short Term Fluctuations in U.S. Voting Behavior, 1896–1964"; and Edward R. Tufte, "Determinants of the Outcomes of Midterm Congressional Elections."

50. Fair, "The Effect of Economic Events on Votes for President."

51. Markus, "The Impact of Personal and National Economic Conditions on the Presidential Vote: A Pooled Cross-Sectional Analysis."

52. Stanley G. Kelley, *Interpreting Elections* (Princeton, N.J.: Princeton University Press, 1983).

53. Ian Budge and Dennis Farlie, *Predicting Elections: Issue Effects and Party Strategies in Twenty-three Democracies* (London: George Allen and Unwin, 1983).

54. Harold Clarke, Kai Hildebrandt, Lawrence LeDuc and Jon Pammett, "Issue Volatility and Partisan Linkages in Canada, Great Britain, The United States, and West Germany," *European Journal of Political Research,* 13 (1985), pp. 237–263.

55. Harold D. Clarke, Jane Jenson, Lawrence LeDuc and Jon H. Pammett, *Political Choice in Canada* (Toronto: McGraw-Hill Ryerson Ltd., 1979).

56. Harold D. Clarke, Jane Jenson, Lawrence LeDuc, and Jon H. Pammett, *Absent Mandate* (Toronto: Gage Publishing, Ltd., 1984), ch. 6.

57. Allan Kornberg and Harold D. Clarke, "Canada's Tory Tide: Electoral Change and Partisan Instability in the 1980s," in Barry Cooper, Allan Kornberg and William Mishler, eds., *The Resurgence of Conservatism in Anglo-American Democracies* (Durham: Duke University Press, 1988), pp. 351–386.

58. Kelley, *Interpreting Elections.*

59. G. Bingham Powell, Jr., "Models of Citizen Control Through Elections," paper presented to the American Political Science Association, Washington, D.C., 1986.

60. Powell, "Models of Citizen Control Through Elections."

61. See Richard Brody and Benjamin Page, "The Assessment of Policy Voting," *American Political Science Review,* 66 (1972), pp. 459–465.

62. "Problems or Voting Issues? A Perspective on Public Perceptions," *Public Opinion* (July/August 1988). It is also pointed out that other issues, such as the appropriate role of government in various spheres of activity, have been translated into images of the respective parties. They cite the case of public welfare. Voters who favor a larger government role in social welfare would favor the Democrats since that party has long been associated with that position.

63. It might be suggested that the *validated* vote measure should be used rather than the *reported* vote variable. However, there may be major problems with the validated measure. The 1984 Michigan CPS study was the first instance in which individuals were trained to check voting and registration records. The *validated* vote for 1984 was 68 percent, only 6 percent different from *reported* vote. In contrast, previous validated vote figures showed a 15–18 point discrepancy with reported vote, suggesting that many voters may well have been included in the non-validated category when in fact they did vote. Further, this would suggest either that the sampling procedure produces a population skewed toward the higher SES groups—hence selecting a population with a greater proclivity to vote—or, the surveys represent an intervention in that the interviewing process acts to encourage respondents to vote. In reality, of course, the results are likely to be a combination of these factors.

In addition to these theoretical problems, the 1972 validation was severely damaged by the fact that efforts were not made to validate the 1972 vote until November 1977, which greatly reduced the ability of researchers to track down records, etc.

In practical terms for this study, the differences in reported and validated vote vis-a-vis candidates was trivial. The negative effect of using validated measures was the reduction in the number of issue responses.

64. One approach suggests that when party identification is included in a voting model, one should use respondent's partisanship lagged one period. The justification is that contemporaneous party identification is a function not only of previous party identification but also current retrospective evaluations of party performance, issue positions, and candidate evaluations. This model tries to control for partisan endogenity. I have chosen to use contemporaneous partisanship, as is still commonly done in voting studies. From a practical standpoint, panel studies are the only accurate means of assessing changes in party identification. Using this approach would have limited me to use of the 1972–76 period.

65. Also, we would generally expect mediated issue effects to be stronger than simple unmediated effects, since the former attribute responsibility to a political entity. For a discussion, see Fiorina, Ch. 6. Also Mark N. Peffley, "The Voter As Juror: Attributing Responsibility for Economic Conditions." *Political Behavior,* 6: (1984), pp. 275–294.

66. This requires use of respondents' answers to their vote in the previous election. Respondents have a tendency to misreport previous vote. The problem can be dealt with using panel data, but this is only available for 1972–76. See Aage, R. Clausen, "Response Validity and Vote Report," *Public Opinion Quarterly,* 32 (1968–69), pp. 588–606; and Blair J. Weir, "The Distortion of Voter Recall," *American Journal of Political Science,* 59 (1975), pp. 53–62.

Chapter 3

1. Gallup Opinion Index, July 1971.

2. Gallup Opinion Index, August 1972, p. 2. The last survey prior to the election using the presidential approval question was July of 1972.

3. U.S. Bureau of Labor Statistics, *Monthly Labor Review,* January 1969–December 1972.

4. Gallup Opinion Index, January 1972.

5. Gallup Opinion Index, March 1972.

6. Stephen Wayne, *The Road to the White House* (New York: St. Martin's Press, 1984).

7. Token Republican opposition consisted of Ohio Congressman John Ashbrook, who was considered to the right of Nixon, partially owing to his Salt I Treaty opposition; and Congressman Peter McCloskey of California, who opposed Nixon's handling of the Vietnam War.

8. Gallup Opinion Index, April 1972.

9. Gallup Opinion Index, August 1972.

10. Edward R. Tufte, *Political Control of the Economy.*

11. Gallup Opinion Index, June 1972.

12. Gallup Opinion Index, September 1972.

13. Herbert R. Asher, *Presidential Elections and American Politics* (Homewood, Ill.: Dorsey Press, 1984), p. 141.

14. Gallup Opinion Index, October 1972.

15. As I noted in Chapter Two, Budge and Farlie find in *Explaining and Predicting Elections* that parties "own" certain issues. Conservative parties have advantages on issues such as crime and inflation. Thus, a simple reward-punishment model may be inapplicable in the U.S. for issues other than the economy and an issue-priority effect present in a number of issue areas.

16. Walter Dean Burnham, *Critical Elections and the Mainspring of American Politics* (New York: W. W. Norton, 1970).

17. Angus Campbell, "Surge and Decline: A Study of Electoral Change," in Angus Campbell, Philip E. Converse, Warren E. Miller and Donald Stokes, eds., *Elections and the Political Order* (New York: Wiley, 1966), pp. 63–77.

18. See Key, *The Responsible Electorate,* for an analysis using similar techniques.

Chapter 4

1. Gallup Opinion Index, January 1976.
2. Taken from Gallup Opinion Index, July 1976, p. 3. The last survey prior to the election using the presidential approval question was July, 1976.
3. U.S. Bureau of Labor Statistics, *Monthly Labor Review*, January 1973–December 1976.
4. Gallup Opinion Index, January 1976.
5. Gallup Opinion Index, February 1976.
6. Gallup Opinion Index, December 1976.
7. James David Barber, *The Pulse of Politics* (New York: W.W. Norton, 1980), p. 191.
8. Gallup Opinion Index, December 1976.
9. Gallup Opinion Index, June 1976.
10. Gallup Opinion Index, June 1976.
11. Gallup Opinion Index, September 1976.
12. Gallup Opinion Index, November 1976.
13. Asher, *Presidential Elections and American Politics.*
14. Carter has been described as the most conservative Democratic president of the twentieth century, given his relatively lukewarm support for major new social welfare initiatives. Yet, it also seems clear that Carter faced an array of economic constraints with which previous Democratic presidents had not had to deal.
15. Rosenstone, *Forecasting Presidential Elections.*
16. The simultaneous presence of inflation and unemployment is known as "stagflation" and provided a severe challenge to the basic tenets of Keynesianism. It was the presence of stagflation, together with the challenge to the dominant Keynesian orthodoxy, which provided an opportunity for monetarist and supply-side theories to gain credence.
17. Unweighted samples are used in the 1976 cross-sectional study. However, differences between the weighted and unweighted analyses were relatively trivial. The panel study is self-weighted.
18. The crime-disorder variable had to be dropped from this part of the analysis because its inclusion prevented the obtaining of an adequate maximum likelihood solution. This may have been due to the fact the frequency distribution was excessively skewed and/or problems of multicollinearity. Regarding the last point, correlation coefficients did not reveal especially high correlations between crime and the other variables, although this would not tell us if multicollinearity existed whereby one variable is represented by a linear combination of other variables.
19. Alt, *The Politics of Economic Decline.*

Chapter 5

1. Christopher J. Deering and Steven J. Smith, "Subcommittees in Congress," in Lawrence C. Dodd and Bruce I. Oppenheimer, eds., *Congress Reconsidered* (Washington, D.C.: Congressional Quarterly Press, 1985), pp. 189–210.

2. It should be recalled from my earlier discussion in Chapter 2 concerning issue priorities that they are based on perceptions voters have of the relative concerns of the two parties and that these perceptions would appear to be grounded in macroeconomic reality. Stimulative fiscal and monetary policies early in the Carter administration certainly risked fueling higher inflation. See Donald F. Kettle, *Leadership at the Fed* (New Haven: Yale University Press, 1986), chapter 7. Also see John T. Woolley, "Partisan Manipulation of the Economy: Another Look at Monetary Policy With Moving Regressions," *Journal Of Politics*, 50 (1988), pp. 3–64.

3. Walter Dean Burnham, "The 1980 Earthquake: Realignment, Reaction, or What?" in Thomas Ferguson and Joel Rogers, eds., *The Hidden Election* (New York: Pantheon Books, 1980), pp. 3–64.

4. Gallup data obtained from Gallup Opinion Index, December 1980.

5. Inflation and unemployment data were obtained from the U.S. Bureau of Labor Statistics, *Monthly Labor Review*, January 1977 to December 1980.

6. Richard Harwood, "On the Eve: Americans 1980," in Richard Harwood, ed., *The Pursuit of the Presidency* (New York: Washington-Post Berkeley Books, 1980), pp. 3–18.

7. Harwood, "On the Eve: Industry," in *The Pursuit of the Presidency*.

8. T. R. Reid, "Scramble: The Primaries—Kennedy," *The Pursuit of the Presidency*.

9. Gallup Opinion Index, December 1979.

10. Gallup Opinion Index, February 1980.

11. Michael Malbin, "The Democrats: A Platform That Carter May Find Awkward to Stand On," *National Journal*, 12 (1980), pp. 1389–1390.

12. Gallup Opinion Index, September 1980.

13. In fact, as events were to prove, Reagan's clear priorities in his first term—and afterwards—were his economic agenda, though he paid lip service to his "social issue" constituency.

Chapter 6

1. Austin Ranney, "Reagan's First Term," in Austin Ranney, ed., *The American Elections of 1984* (Durham, N.C.: Duke University Press, 1985), pp. 1–35.

2. Paul R. Abramson, John H. Aldrich, and David W. Rohde, *Change and Continuity in the 1984 Elections* (Washington, D.C.: Congressional Quarterly Press, 1986), pp. 133–156.

3. William Schneider, "The November 6 Vote for President: What Did It Mean?" in *The American Elections of 1984*, pp. 203–244.

4. Nelson Polsby, "The Democratic Nomination and the Evolution of the Party System," in *The American Elections of 1984*, pp. 36–65.

5. This reflects what Schneider (see note 3) refers to as a "presidential" realignment.

6. Polsby, p. 45.

7. A comparison with other presidents shows that even at the height of his popularity in May 1981 (just following the March 31 assassination attempt and the Reagan budget victory in Congress) it was still not as high as that obtained by presidents Eisenhower and Kennedy at the end of their first four months.

Gallup surveys showed Eisenhower and Kennedy with approval ratings of 74 and 75 percent, respectively, at the end of their first four months in office.

8. Gallup poll data were obtained from the Gallup Opinion Index, December 1984.

9. Data for inflation and unemployment were obtained from the U.S. Bureau of Labor Statistics, *Monthly Labor Review*, January 1981 to December 1984.

10. Ranney, pp. 21–22.

11. Gallup Opinion Index, selected issues January–May 1982.

12. Ranney, p. 21.

13. Paul E. Peterson, "The New Politics of Deficits," in John E. Chubb and Paul E. Peterson, eds., *The New Direction in American Politics* (Washington, D.C.: The Brookings Institution, 1985), pp. 365–398.

14. Gallup Opinion Index, August 1983.

15. As noted earlier, Reagan certainly seemed to recognize the electoral value of the social issue constituency, but never placed their issue concerns at the top of his agenda. Relatedly, social concerns such as abortion, affirmative action, and the like were mentioned by only miniscule proportions of those surveyed in a variety of polls.

16. However, the value of the Hart and Glenn appeals were different. While Hart was quite consciously seeking the support of the so-called yuppie (young, urban, upwardly mobile, professional constituency) or "new generation," Glenn sought what might be referred to as the "silent majority" of moderate to moderate-conservative Democratic primary voters.

17. Gallup Opinion Index, December 1982.

18. Michael J. Robinson, "Where's the Beef? Media and Media Elites in 1984," in *The American Elections of 1984*.

19. It is difficult to assess the influence Jackson had upon the Democratic contest for the nomination and upon the more general dynamics of the 1984 campaign. Jackson did activate many blacks who may otherwise not have participated, but his candidacy may also have had a "backlash" effect in that it stimulated decreased white registration and voting in the South.

20. Charles O. Jones in *The American Elections of 1984*, pp. 66–100.

21. Elizabeth Drew, *Campaign Journal* (New York: MacMillan, 1985), pp. 581–582.

22. This attack came immediately after the Democratic convention. In a speech at Austin, Texas, President Reagan hammered repeatedly at the tax issue. Besides using the quote above, the President went on to say "Our friends in the other party have never met a tax they didn't like—didn't like, or didn't hike." Quoted in the *Congressional Quarterly Weekly Report*, August 25, 1984, p. 2123.

23. Here is an instance in which the deficit, seemingly a valence-type issue which should have worked against the incumbents, can be neutralized by pointing out that Democratic solutions required tax increases. Similarly, emphasis on the budget deficit reduced the ability of the Democrats to offer the hope of significant increases in social welfare "New Deal" programs targeted at substantially Democratic constituencies.

24. Albert R. Hunt, "The Campaign and the Issues," in Ranney, pp. 129–165.

25. Paul R. Abramson, et al., pp. 57–60.

26. Schneider, in Ranney, pp. 203–244.

27. Philip E. Converse, "The Concept of a Normal Vote," in Angus Campbell, et al.

28. Several works make this argument. See, for instance, Abramson, et al., ch. 7.

Chapter 7

1. Clarke, et al., *Absent Mandate: The Politics of Discontent in Canada*, ch. 8.

2. Alt, *The Politics of Economic Decline*, ch. 1. Alt also suggests that expectations will play a role in determining the effect of economic influences on election outcomes.

3. William H. Riker, "Political Theory and the Art of Heresthetics," in Ada W. Finifter, ed., *Political Science: The State of the Discipline* (Washington, D.C.: American Political Science Association, 1983), pp. 63–64. Here, heresthetics is defined as the manipulation of tastes and alternatives within which decisions are made.

4. Edward G. Carmines and James A. Stimson, "The Dynamics of Issue Evolution in the United States," in Richard Niemi and Herbert Weisberg, eds., *Electoral Change in Advanced Industrial Democracies* (Princeton: Princeton University Press, 1984), pp. 134–158.

5. Clarke, et al., *Absent Mandate*, ch. 8.

6. Michel J. Crozier, Samuel P. Huntington and Joji Watanuki, *The Crisis of Democracy* (New York: New York University Press, 1975).

7. Peter Bachrach and Morton Baratz, "The Two Faces of Power," *American Political Science Review*, 56 (1962), pp. 947-952.

8. Edward G. Carmines, Steven H. Renten and James A. Stimson, "Events and Alignments: The Party Image Link," in Richard Niemi and Herbert Weisberg, eds., *Controversies in Voting Behavior* (Washington, D.C.: Congressional Quarterly Press, 1984), ch. 6.

9. Page, *Choices and Echoes in Presidential Elections*, pp. 545–560.

10. Kenneth A. Shepsle, "The Strategy of Ambiguity: Uncertainty and Electoral Competition," *American Political Science Review*, 66 (1972), pp. 558–568.

11. Budge and Farlie, *Explaining and Predicting Elections*, p. 144.

Chapter 8

1. "Bob Dole's Furies," *Newsweek*, November 21, 1988, pp. 87–88.

2. "Don't Worry, Be Happy," *Newsweek*, November 21, 1988, pp. 84–85.

3. See the Gallup Opinion surveys for an examination of trends in presidential popularity. Also, see *Public Opinion*, Jan./Feb. 1989, Washington, D.C.: American Enterprise Institute, pp. 36–40 for popularity trends of all recent presidents.

4. Douglas A. Hasbrecht and Richard Fly, "For Bush, A Moment of Truth in New Hampshire," *Business Week*, February 22, 1988, p. 28. Also see "Iowa and After," *National Review*, March 4, 1988.

5. "Elephants on Parade," *Newsweek*, November 21, 1988, pp. 92–94.

6. Steven W. Colford, "How Dole Killed Election Hopes," *Advertising Age*, (59) March 7, 1988, p. 1.

7. Richard Fly and Douglas Hasbrecht (with Paul Magnusson and Scott Ticer, Tim Scott and Gail DeGeorge), "George Bush's Knockout Punch," *Business Week*, March 21, 1988, p. 44.

8. "Looking for Mr. Right," *Newsweek*, November 21, 1988, p. 35. Also, for a retrospective on Gary Hart's difficulties see "Fatal Attraction," same issue.

9. See, for example, Rod Paul, "The Field Narrows as New Hampshire Votes—Bush and Dukakis," *Nation's City Weekly*, 7, February 22, 1988, p. 1. For an especially interesting article on the Dukakis-Gephardt battle, see Walter Shapiro, "Battling for the Post-liberal Soul," *Time*, February 22, 1988, pp. 19–21.

10. Walter Shapiro, "Three-Way Gridlock," *Time*, March 21, 1988, p. 22.

11. For an excellent discussion of resource allocation strategies and the influence of candidates' competitiveness on such strategies, see Paul-Henri Gurian, "Resource Allocation Strategies in Presidential Nomination Campaigns," *American Journal of Political Science* (1986), pp. 802–821.

12. For an excellent survey of national as well as state polls, from which this data was taken, see *Public Opinion*, November-December, (Washington, D.C.: American Enterprise Institute, 1988), pp. 36–40.

13. *Public Opinion*, November-December (1988), p. 37.

14. *Public Opinion*, November-December (1988), p. 37.

15. There was evidence of a last minute surge by Dukakis in midwestern industrial states which appears to have cut Bush's overall victory margin. See E. J. Donne, Jr., "A Late Drive by Dukakis Fails Despite a Surge in Industrial Areas," *New York Times*, November 9, 1988, p. 1.

16. For an analysis of the election outcome, see Thomas B. Edsall and Richard Morris, *Washington Post*, November 9, pp. 28–29.

17. R. W. Apple, Jr., "Political Experts Offer 3 Views of '88 Election," *New York Times*, October 29, 1988, p. 10L.

18. This is the view expressed by John Petrocik, who refers to the 1988 election as a "confirming" election. See R. W. Apple, Jr., *New York Times*, October 29, 1988, p. 10L. Petrocik's view, of course, is a variant of a theme expressed by several writers who suggest that long-term structural forces are contributing to a Republican realignment, at least at the presidential level. One view expressed by John Chubb and Paul E. Peterson is that the Electoral College provides a distinct advantage to the Republican presidential candidate. This is because the Republican's strength tends to be concentrated in larger states, hence each electoral vote captured by the Republicans in these states is won with fewer popular votes than necessary to win electoral votes in larger states. Second, the Republicans have built a block of states in the South and West increasingly viewed as "safe" for their candidate. See Chubb and Peterson, "Realignment and Institutionalization," in *The New Direction in American Politics*, John Chubb and Paul E. Peterson, eds. (Washington, D.C.: The Brookings Institution, 1986), pp. 1–30. One might also add that many of those states which the Republicans seemingly have a "lock" are also those gaining in population, and consequently in electoral votes. This is also a view expressed by political consultant Horace Busby as well as William Schneider's theory of a realignment only at the presidential level. See Schneider, *The American Elections of 1984*. More generally, the importance of long-term historical forces is seen in V. O. Key's (1955) classic

work "A Theory of Critical Elections," *Journal of Politics* (17), pp. 3–18, and Angus Campbell's "A Classification of Presidential Elections" in Angus Campbell, et al., *Elections and the Political Order,* pp. 63–77.

19. This is certainly not to suggest that long-term forces don't play a role. Even those associated with the critical or realigning election approach recognize that short-term forces may occasionally influence an outcome in a manner that leads to the majority party's defeat.

20. See, for instance Marie D. Natali, "President Bush or President Dukakis," *Presidential Studies Quarterly,* 18 (1988), pp. 707–716. Also, See James David Barber's *The Presidential Character,* (Englewood Cliffs, N.J.: Prentice-Hall Inc., 1969), for a comprehensive analysis of the impact of character on presidential performance in the White House.

21. Trends on inflation and unemployment are in U.S. Bureau of Labor Statistics, *Monthly Labor Review* (various volumes). Trends on interest rates can be found in *Federal Reserve Bulletin* and Department of Commerce's *Survey of Current Business.*

22. See Ch. 2 for an earlier discussion of Downs's analysis of the decision rules used by the electorate.

23. Thomas B. Edsall and Richard Morin, "Reagan's 1984 Voter Coalition is weakened in Bush Victory," *Washington Post,* November 9, 1988, p. A31.

24. See *Public Opinion,* January/February 1989, p. 33. This information was taken from the ABC News/*Washington Post* exit poll, November 8, 1988. This issue also reports findings from a CBS News/*New York Times* survey of November 10–16, 1988, in which 45 percent of the respondents indicated their belief that it would not be necessary to raise taxes, while 38 percent believed it would be necessary. In addition, 64 percent said that the new president shouldn't ask Congress for a tax increase while 31 percent said he should raise taxes.

25. *New York Times*–CBS News exit poll, as reported in *New York Times,* November 9, 1988.

26. Thomas Edsall and Richard Morin, *Washington Post,* p. A31.

27. Edsall and Morin, pp. A30–31.

28. Edsall and Morin, pp. A30–31.

29. See for instance R. W. Apple, "Challenges for Bush: Agenda and Congress," *New York Times,* November 9, 1988, p. B1, also Tom Wicker, "Sowing the Whirlwind," *New York Times,* November 9, 1988, p. B1.

Appendix B

1. John Aldrich and Forrest Nelson, *Linear Probability, Logit and Probit Models* (Berkeley: Sage Publications, 1982).

2. Richard M. McKelvey and William Zavoina, "An IBM Fortran IV Program to Perform N-Chotomous Multivariate Probit Analysis," *Behavioral Science,* 16 (1971), pp. 186–187.

3. See Fiorina, pp. 213–224.

Index